The Unseen Realities of God's Kingdom

By

Dr. Shirley Christian

Unless otherwise indicated, all scripture is from the New American Standard Bible, copyright 1960, 1962, 1963, 1968, 1971, 1972, 1973, 1975, 1977, 1995 by the Lockman Foundation, Used by Permission.

The Unseen Realities of
God's Kingdom
Copyright © May 2008
Shirley Christian Ministries
In Streams of His Grace
ISBN 978-0-6152-3556-1

www.shirleychristian.org

All rights in this book are reserved. No part may be reproduced in any manner without permission in writing from the publisher, except in brief quotations used in connection with a review in a magazine or newspaper.

Table of Contents

INTRODUCTION..6
                 The Keys of the Kingdom..8

Chapter One   The Kingdom of Heaven and the Kingdom of God—The Definition...13

Chapter Two   The Kingdom is Breaking Forth and Advancing........25
                 The Kingdom is Power 29

Chapter Three   The First Kingdom 34
                 The Principle of God's
                 Presence and Sovereignty 39

Chapter Four   The Age to Come...42
                 The Powers of the Age to Come 46

Chapter Five   The Present Age...52
                 The Grace of the Kingdom 54
                 The Kingdom First...56
                 The Value of the Kingdom of Heaven........................59

Chapter Six   Kingdom Living Keys..62
                 The Kingdom Love Key 67

Chapter Seven Keys that Continue to Unlock Big Doors...................74
                 The Kingdom Faith Key 79
                 The Kingdom Joy Key 85
                 The Kingdom Peace Key...86
                 The Kingdom Hope Key..87
                 The Kingdom Humility Key 88
                 The Kingdom Wisdom Key 89

Chapter Eight The Narrow Entrance into the Kingdom 91
                 The Great Invitations 92
                 Repentance is a Kingdom Key 95
                 Forgiveness is a Kingdom Key 98

Chapter Nine Mysteries of the Kingdom 102
                 Parable of the Sower 106

CONCLUSION ....
                 The Master Key—Covenant of the Kingdom 111
                 Covenant Inheritance 114
                 The Kingdom Keyless Entry 116

BIBLIOGRAPHY 118

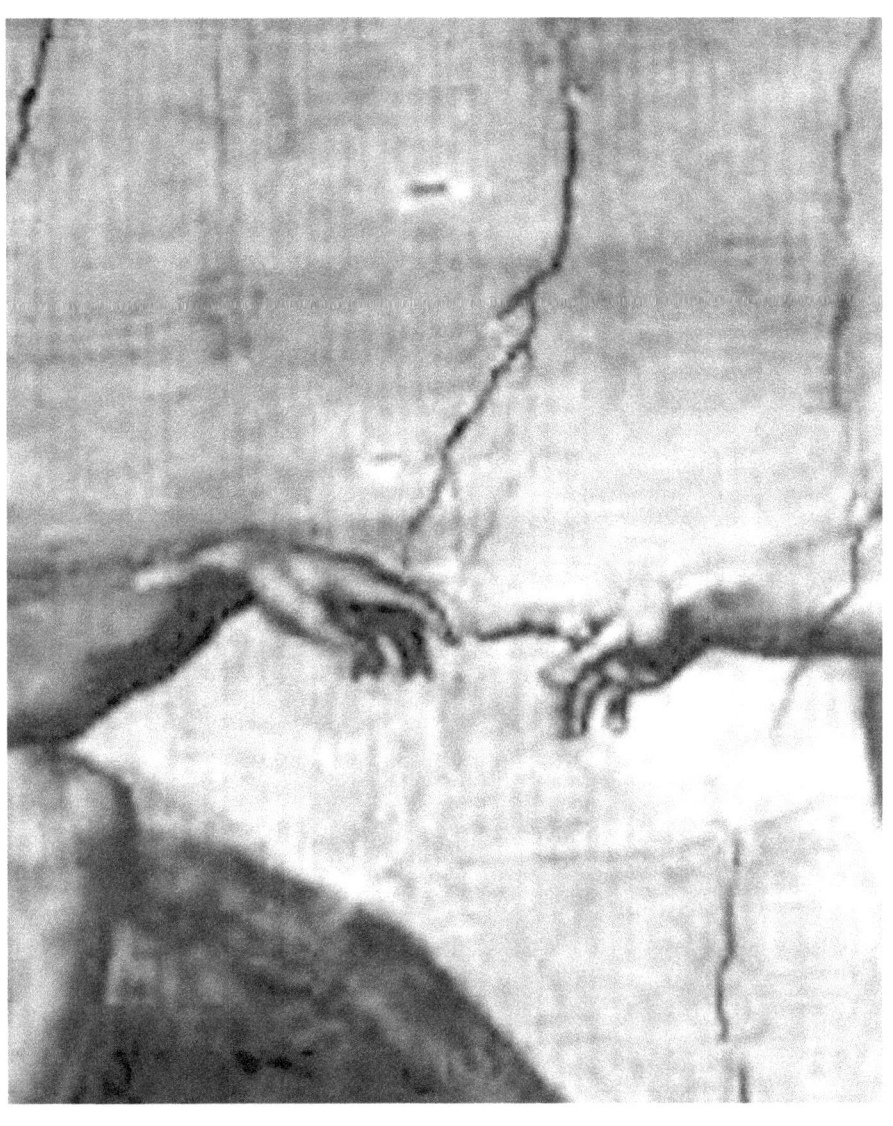

"From the days of John the Baptist until now the Kingdom of Heaven is breaking through, and those who break through seize it." (Matthew 11:12)

THE UNSEEN REALITIES OF GOD'S KINGDOM

INTRODUCTION

The Kingdom of Heaven stands out significantly in Jesus Christ's focus and teaching. He relates His mission to the Kingdom, and His apostles after Him, including Paul, preached the Kingdom. Jesus wanted His followers to embrace this message, so He gave many illustrations, parables, and encouragement on entering the Kingdom, and what the Kingdom is like. However, Jewish believers who anticipated the coming of Messiah expected the Messiah to restore Israel—set up the eternal kingdom, both political and spiritual. When Jesus demonstrated the power of the Kingdom, their expectation heightened so that they looked to its immediate fulfillment. John's gospel says, "Therefore when Jesus perceived that they were about to come and take Him by force to make Him king, He departed again to the mountain by Himself alone" (John 6:15).

After His death and resurrection, Jesus appeared to His followers "during forty days and speaking of the things pertaining to the kingdom of God" (Acts 1:3). The Kingdom had been such a strong force and focus during His ministry and afterwards, that one of His disciples' first questions was about the Kingdom: "And so when they had come together, they were asking Him, saying, Lord, is it at this time You are restoring the kingdom to Israel?'" (Acts 1:6). Their questions focused on an immediate earthly expression of the Kingdom that Jesus had so vehemently taught and demonstrated. To them, the Kingdom was one of eschatological significance, when the Son of Man came and Israel once again became a Kingdom of self-rule under its Great Prince. Even the thief on the cross beside Jesus had knowledge of the rabbinic concept of the Kingdom of Heaven. He cried, "Lord, remember me when You come into Your kingdom" (Luke 23:42). One can see that Jesus' primary message so encompassed this concept of Kingdom that His followers longingly looked to its consummation at any moment.

To fully grasp the teachings of Jesus about the Kingdom of Heaven, it is necessary to look at them from His own historic Judaic heritage. The Kingdom is deeply rooted in the consciousness of the Jewish people, and it has both an historical basis and a spiritual basis. Contrary to what you may have heard or been taught, when Jesus speaks of "the Kingdom," the difference between the Kingdom of God and the Kingdom of Heaven is non-existent! Jesus did not speak of two different kingdoms, but one. For example, Matthew's gospel, which appears addressed more to the Jews, uses the "Kingdom of Heaven," and Luke's gospel, when translated into Greek for the Gentiles, expresses the Kingdom as the "Kingdom of God." To hold God's name in awe and avoid any vain use of it, the Jews substituted "Heaven" for "God." This was a frequent euphemism. Today, many still say, the Name, *HaShem*, and they leave the "o" out of God when they write it.

> *The difference between the Kingdom of God and the Kingdom of Heaven is Non-existent!*

As did many of His contemporaries during the second Temple period, Jesus avoided using God's name lightly, and often, He substituted "Heaven" for "God." Jesus had much in common with other rabbis of this period, but His focus and understanding of the Kingdom sets Him apart. Thus, Jesus and the sages before Him used "Heaven" as a synonym for "God," and the term is interchangeable with "God."

It further helps to understand that the "Kingdom of Heaven," the *Malkut Shamayim* in Hebrew, is a rabbinical expression and is found primarily in the writings of the sages and in the New Testament, but not in the Old Testament. Just because the term is not found in the Old Testament does not mean that it was not a concept well understood by Jesus and His fellow Jews, who valued the oral word on much the same level with the written word. A quick word search of the Old Testament brings up "kingdom" often, but not the rabbinic concept of the Kingdom of Heaven.

> *The "Kingdom of Heaven," the Malkut Shamayim in Hebrew, is a rabbinical expression and is found in the New Testament and writings of the sages, but not in the Old Testament.*

Jesus, a Rabbi and a prophet, and yet much more, would have known the sages' writings well, and His teachings often reflect the wisdom of this vast source of knowledge. Typical study for a Jewish child consisted of: "at five (or at six) Bible (Tanach); at ten Mishna; at fifteen Talmud" (Jewish Encyclopedia). The Jews committed these sources to memory, a concept hard for us to visualize!

It is important to note that the "oral teachings" existed before and after the time of Jesus. The written Torah was often interpreted further by the Oral Torah, which covered a period of several hundred years. It was considered as authoritative as the written Torah by the Pharisees, of whom Jesus' teachings are more closely aligned.

If you are not familiar with the terms, Torah, Mishnah, Talmud and Tanach, they mean: *Torah*—first five books of the Bible; *Tanach*—the Old Testament made up of the Torah (Pentateuch), Prophets, and writings (from the first letters of Torah, Neviim, and Ketuvin); *Mishna*—the collection of oral teachings (Oral Torah) put into writing in approximately 200 A.D.; *Talmud*—commentary on the Mishna. Jews within Israel and Jews in the Diaspora each wrote a Talmud. The one from the Diaspora is called the Babylonian Talmud. It is considered more authoritative—put into writing about 500 A.D.

THE KEYS OF THE KINGDOM

Jesus compared the preacher or teacher who understands, interprets, and teaches on the Kingdom with the head of a house who draws on the personal treasure he has accumulated. The treasure is a reference to the biblical texts from the Old Testament, and Jesus' new teachings on the Kingdom of Heaven. The Scriptures are a treasure, preserved for us by God's people. The Lord said,

> And He said to them, "Therefore every scribe who has become a disciple of the kingdom of heaven is like a head of a household, who brings forth out of his treasure things new and old." (Matt. 13:52)

Jesus said the Scriptures were intact, certain, and would stand until all was fulfilled: "For assuredly, I say to you, till heaven and earth pass away, one jot or one tittle will by no means pass from the law till all is fulfilled" (Matt 5:18). The Old Testament, the old wine men prefer (Luke 5:39), is a storehouse of treasure. As to His words to His generation, He said, "The heaven and the earth shall pass away, but My Words shall not pass away" (Luke 21:33). We all agree the Bible is God-breathed; the Spirit of God inspired it. "The words that I speak to you are spirit and are life" (John 6:63). The point is: God's Spirit inspires the whole of the Bible, as are the words of Jesus. They will not pass away. They are a great treasure, as are the words of the Old Testament. They are one. According to Bible expositor Adam Clarke:

> (The treasure) may also refer to the old and new covenants—a proper knowledge of the Old Testament Scriptures, and of the doctrines of Christ as contained in the New . . . Every scribe: Minister of Christ: who is instructed-taught of God; in the kingdom of heaven—in the mysteries of the Gospel of Christ: out of his treasury—his granary or storehouse; things new and old—a Jewish phrase for great plenty . . . His knowledge consists in being well instructed in the things concerning the kingdom of heaven, and the art of conducting men . . . The law is still a schoolmaster to lead men to Christ—by it is the knowledge of sin, and, without it, there can be no conviction. (Clarke Matt 13:52)

Jesus taught from His broad Knowledge of the sages and the Scriptures, and He gave the "Keys of the Kingdom" to Peter and those who follow Him in confessing, "You are the Christ, the Son of the God Who Lives" (Matt 16:16-19). The Keys He gave were not about binding and loosing devils; we just cast them out. Jesus was talking about correctly interpreting scripture authoritatively. Jesus made Peter both steward and judge with the keys, the one who can prohibit and permit (bind and loose). Keys represent authority, and keys opened the treasury of the king. In Revelation Jesus said, "I have the keys to death and hell," representing authority over death and hell. Therefore, prohibit and permit is the understood meaning of to bind and loose.

Peter did not ask the Lord what He meant when He gave Kingdom Keys, because in his day, it was a common term. In Judaism, binding and loosing is a legal designation—to bind or prohibit certain activities and loose or allow others. Again, it is about interpreting scripture and permitting or prohibiting certain actions, determining what is legal or illegal.

Jesus accused the party of the Pharisees with not "loosing" the burdens they laid on the shoulders of men, and of "binding" burdens on them (Matt 23:2-4). He wanted the fullness of the Word of God to become not a burden, but a joy. He said, "Do not think that I came to abolish the Law or the Prophets; I did not come to abolish, but to fulfill" (Matt. 5:17). To fulfill the law was to correctly interpret it, and to abolish the law was to misinterpret. The Keys of the Kingdom are for correctly interpreting the Scriptures, and for then binding or loosing.

Jesus spoke with authority, unlike the scribes and Pharisees who claimed the right to interpret the Scriptures (Mark 1:27). Jesus also exercised authority to forgive sins, something that set His contemporaries on edge: "And the scribes and the Pharisees began to reason, saying, "Who is this man who speaks blasphemies? Who can forgive sins, but God alone?" (Luke 5:21). When Jesus says, "I will give you the keys of the kingdom of heaven; and whatever you shall bind on earth shall be bound in heaven, and whatever you shall loose on earth shall be loosed in heaven" (Matt. 16:19), He was declaring that the Keys of the Kingdom provide authority to decide an issue, and Heaven backs it up. Heaven is the spiritual realm. What we declare in the earth is what is done in the spiritual realm when we are in right standing with the King and use the Keys to the Kingdom.

> *What we declare in the earth is what is done in the spiritual realm when we are in right-standing with the King, and use the Keys to the Kingdom.*

The spiritual realm is the pattern for the physical realm. And the spiritual realm fulfills what those with this authority key declare on earth. No wonder Jesus said, "If you had faith like a mustard seed, you would say to this mulberry tree, 'Be uprooted and be planted in the sea'; and it would obey you'" (Luke 17:6). The unseen realities of the Kingdom of Heaven govern the natural. We live in both dimensions at one time. The Jewish understanding of Jesus' use of this term follows:

> The power or right of deciding the Law, in dubious cases, or of interpreting, modifying, or amplifying, and occasionally of abrogating it, as vested in the Rabbis as its teachers and expounders. The Pharisees always claimed the power of binding and loosing. The various schools had the power "to bind and to loose"; that is, to forbid and to permit (•ag. 3b); and they could bind any day by declaring it a fast-day (Meg. Ta'an. xxii.; Ta'an. 12a; Yer. Ned. i. 36c, d). By these words he (Jesus) virtually invested them with the same authority as that which he found belonging to the scribes and Pharisees who "bind heavy burdens and lay them on men's shoulders, but will not move them with one of their fingers"; that is, "loose them," as they have the power to do (Matt. xxiii. 2-4). In the same sense, in the second epistle of Clement to James II. ("Clementine Homilies," Introduction), Peter is represented as having appointed Clement as his successor, saying: "I communicate to him the power of binding and loosing so that, with respect to everything which he shall ordain in the earth, it shall be decreed in the heavens; for he shall bind what ought to be bound and loose what ought to be loosed as knowing the rule of the church." Quite different from this Judaic and ancient view of the apostolic power of binding and loosing is the one expressed in John xx. 23, where Jesus is represented as having said to his disciples after they had received the Holy Spirit: "Whosoever sins ye remit, they are remitted unto them; and whosoever sins ye retain, they are retained." It is this view, which, adopted by Tertullian and all the church fathers, invested the head of the Christian Church with the power to forgive sins, the "clavis ordinis," "the key-power of the Church." (Jewish Encyclopedia)

The book of Acts gives an example of the early disciples' use of the authority the Lord gave to bind and loose. They used the keys of the kingdom to open the door for Gentiles into the Kingdom of Heaven without requiring them to fulfill all of the Law, including circumcision. Circumcision is the sign God gave Abraham of Covenant, but it is only part of the Jewish Covenant; however some Judaizers required converts to keep this requirement. The early church ruled not to require converts to be circumcised (Acts 15:13-20). When "two or three agree," it is backed up by heaven. This applies to interpretation and using the Keys of the Kingdom. It is a reference to correctly interpreting the scriptures. Why would the prayer of three mean more to God than one's own prayer? True, a corporate anointing is powerful, but agreement of two or three is in the form of interpretation of the law. Two or three witnesses established a fact in a Jewish court of law (Deut. 19:15). Let us use this authority to correctly interpret the scriptures on the Kingdom of Heaven, which is also the Kingdom of God.

Having clarified the correct application of binding and loosing, we must also insist that this interpretation does not in any way negate our authority as believers, the authority to cast out devils, heal the sick and all that we should do as followers of Christ. But it helps to put certain scriptures on more solid ground and our believer's authority on firmer footing when we apply this knowledge accurately. Out of the "the treasure of things new and old," we can look to the historic Jesus and His teachings preserved for us, as can we embrace the Old Testament and the wisdom of the sages.

CHAPTER ONE

THE KINGDOM OF HEAVEN AND THE KINGDOM OF GOD—THE DEFINITION

The Kingdom of Heaven is like . . .

The word "Kingdom" consists of two words, "king" and "dom," which is from domain. Thus a kingdom includes a king and his domain, the realm of his rule. A domain may include the people in it.

The Kingdom of Heaven is at the same time a present spiritual reality and a future reality. To enter the Kingdom that Jesus proclaimed, one also entered eternal life, right standing with God, Covenant, and the blessings of the Kingdom. Our personal entry into the Kingdom cost God His Son, whom He gave freely. Our part and our cost to enter the Kingdom is complete obedience. Jesus said we would have those material things that we need, and the eternal blessings of the kingdom. God chooses to give it freely to those who believe and obey. Jesus tells His disciples:

> But seek for His kingdom, and these things shall be added to you. Do not be afraid, little flock, for your Father has chosen gladly to give you the kingdom. (Luke 12:31-32)

Matthew's version adds that we should seek the Kingdom "first," and God's righteousness. He reports, "But seek first His kingdom and His righteousness; and all these things shall be added to you" (Matt 6:33). Putting this together, we can see that seeking the Kingdom involves more than just an expression of belief, but also a righteous way of living.

God is sovereign and thus, when we speak of God's sovereignty and rule, we must speak in the general sense of God's providential rule over the Universe; He is King of the Universe. He says, "Heaven is my throne and the earth is my footstool" (Isa 66:1); and "For the kingship and the kingdom are the Lord's, and He is the ruler over the nations" (Psalm 22:28 AMP). As to the manifestation of the Kingdom of God on earth, when one comes under God's rule and accepts His commands, and welcomes His rule from the heart, he comes into God's kingdom, which Jesus gave His life to bring into immediate redemptive manifestation, but not full manifestation.

If then, the Kingdom of Heaven primarily refers to God's rule over His people, when He rules in our lives, then we are counted as His own and obey Him, we have come into the Kingdom of Heaven. This is what the Hebrews at Mt. Sinai did after Moses **sprinkled blood** on the people and the book of the law, and the people said, "We will obey." They entered Covenant and the Kingdom of God—His rule:

> Then he took the Book of the Covenant and read in the hearing of the people. And they said, "All that the LORD has said we will do, and be obedient." (Ex. 24:7)

Similar to the Hebrews at Sinai, "Abraham preceded them by accepting the Kingdom and the yoke of God's Torah, when He heard the voice of God and obeyed Him (Book of Jubilees, xii. 19)" (Jewish Encyclopedia). As espoused by the sages and Jesus, God is first in our lives and actions in the Kingdom:

> The last prayer of the daily liturgy in most (Jewish) congregations, so called from its initial word, "'Alenu," which means "It is incumbent upon us," or "It is our duty" includes:
> Before Thee, O Lord our God, shall they kneel and fall down, and unto Thy glorious name give honor. So will they accept the yoke of Thy kingdom, and Thou shall be King over them speedily forever and aye. For Thine is the kingdom, and to all eternity Thou wilt reign in glory, as it is written in Thy Torah: 'The Lord shall reign forever and aye.' And it is also said: 'And the Lord shall be King over all the earth; on that day the Lord shall be One and His name be One' (Jewish Encyclopedia).

Just as in the example of the Abraham and the Hebrews, if we are to be obedient, then we must obey God's voice, His commands and instructions. It amounts to receiving the Kingdom, and agreeing to obey the Lord by taking His yoke. This is the yoke of His instructions and commands. Jesus explained:

> Come to Me, all who labor and are heavy laden, and I will give you rest. Take My yoke upon you and learn from Me, for I am gentle and lowly in heart, and you will find rest for your souls. For My yoke is easy and My burden is light. (Matthew 11:28-30)

When Jesus said, "take my yoke," this term was familiar to most of His contemporaries:

> The Kingdom of God, however, in order to be established on earth, requires recognition by man; that is, to use the Hasidæan phrase borrowed from Babylonia or Persia, man must "take upon himself the yoke of the Kingdom of God." (Jewish Encyclopedia)

Jesus' invitation caused some to take offense and others to act. He so personalized the invitation that He clearly was standing as an authority and as God's own Son. Imagine His listeners hearing a man say, "Take my yoke," when their whole focus on God and "yoke of Torah" consumed their existence. Jesus' words raised many eyebrows. Just who was this brash young Rabbi who spoke so authoritatively on matters only God could command?

> *He will die, and His blood will then be sprinkled on us who obey, so that we can have the free gift of being set-right (right-standing) with God, eternal life, and become partakers with Israel of the Covenant blessings of the Kingdom.*

Jesus is likewise telling His would-be followers, to take His yoke, become His disciple, a learner, and return to Covenant. So what is the essence of what He is saying about His yoke? Are we to believe His yoke is different than the yoke of the written and oral commandments that God gave to His chosen people?

What Jesus is doing amounts to inaugurating and bringing to light a major breakthrough in full manifestation of the redemptive Kingdom. He will die, and His blood will then be sprinkled on us who obey, so that we can have the free gift of being set-right (right-standing) with God, eternal life, and become partakers with Israel of the Covenant blessings of the Kingdom. It is a redemptive Kingdom! In this Kingdom, obedience is such a vital ingredient in expressing Kingdom living. Peter writes:

> Elect according to the foreknowledge of God the Father, in sanctification of the Spirit, **for obedience and sprinkling of the blood of Jesus Christ**. (1Peter 1:2 Emphases added)

Do not esteem lightly this sprinkling of blood. Through a supernatural experience, I saw how receiving the blood of Christ brings protection and immediate change in our spiritual surroundings. Protection is just one aspect of the blood's efficacy, but when one experiences it in such a real way, it is not soon forgotten.

Notice that when Jesus spoke of the Kingdom, He spoke to His fellow Jews who were a "covenant people;" therefore, entering the Kingdom is a covenant decision, which is always ratified by blood. Just as God introduced the law at Sinai through Moses with the blood of covenant, our Lord inaugurated the New Covenant in His blood (Luke 22:20). This Covenant comes with not only the command and instructions our Lord gave us, but with the added ability to keep the Covenant because it comes with the empowerment of His Spirit.

> *The Kingdom of God has come to us in the Person of Jesus Christ. It involves an empowered righteous way of living.*

Thus the Kingdom of God has come to us in the Person of Jesus Christ. It involves an empowered righteous way of living.

Before the cross, we had little hope of entering the Eternal Kingdom. Paul talks about our condition before Christ:

> That at that time you were without Christ, being aliens from the **commonwealth of Israel and strangers from the covenants of promise,** having no hope and without

God in the world. But now in Christ Jesus you who once were far off have been brought near by the blood of Christ. (Ephesians 2:12-13 Emphasis added)

We were once not a part of the commonwealth of Israel. A commonwealth is an entity with civil and religious privileges. It may have a king or ruler, and it includes its citizens. Israel was thought of as having a theocracy. While they asked for an earthly king to govern them and make them more like other nations, God alone was the one worshipped and the "ruler" who had authority to speak and command obedience spiritually.

As to our position as believers in the Lord Jesus, having come into Covenant and entered the Kingdom, of which the root is the commonwealth of Israel and its covenants of great promises, we also enter eternal life. Lest we forget, God promised this New Covenant in the Old. He spoke through Jeremiah and Ezekiel:

> Behold, the days come, says the LORD, that I will make a new covenant with the house of Yisra'el, and with the house of Yehudah: not according to the covenant that I made with their fathers in the day that I took them by the hand to bring them out of the land of Egypt; which my covenant they broke, although I was a husband to them, says the LORD. But this is the covenant that I will make with the house of Yisra'el after those days, says the LORD: I will put my law in their inward parts, and in their heart will I write it; and I will be their God, and they shall be my people: and they shall teach no more every man his neighbor, and every man his brother, saying, Know the LORD; for they shall all know me, from the least of them to the greatest of them, says the LORD: for I will forgive their iniquity, and their sin will I remember no more. (Jer 31:31-34 HNV)

> A new heart also will I give you, and a new spirit will I put within you; and I will take away the stony heart out

of your flesh, and I will give you a heart of flesh. (Eze 36:26 HNV)

Without doubt, God is talking about His covenant people Israel in these verses, but realize, believers in the Lord Jesus have been grafted into the vine, the root being Israel. Paul reminds the church in Rome, made up of mostly Gentiles, of how all Israel will be saved:

> For if you were cut out of that which is by nature a wild olive tree, and were grafted contrary to nature into a good olive tree, how much more will these, which are the natural branches, be grafted into their own olive tree? (Rom 11:24)

In this age, through preaching of the gospel, God has and is bringing in a multitude of Gentile believers into the New Covenant. He has "made us adequate as servants of a new covenant; not of the letter, but of the Spirit. For the letter kills, but the Spirit gives life" (2 Cor 3:6).

Once we believe and are reconciled to God, we enter the Kingdom and real life begins. Eternal life now and in the age to come is ours, as is a new empowered righteous way of living.

Jesus taught that the Kingdom involved more than mere observance of Torah. Yes, His yoke involved more than the yoke of Torah; it went further and deeper, into the very intent of God's words, which the sages so greatly debated. He wanted hearts to be changed, and for the Kingdom to be inclusive of those who were outside the traditional framework of Torah observance. His message resonated in the hearts of the poor, outcasts, sinners, and tax collectors. He said, "I have not come to call the righteous but sinners to repentance" (Luke 5:32). The sages taught, "The yoke of God's Kingdom—the yoke of the Torah—grants freedom from other yokes" (Abot iii. 4) (Jewish Encyclopedia). Jesus

> *We enter the Kingdom through the gate that God provided in Jesus Christ, into salvation, eternal life, and Covenant, and the unseen realities of God's Kingdom begin to be realized in us.*

says, "You will know the truth and the truth will set you free" (John 8:32).

We enter the Kingdom through the gate that God provided in Jesus Christ, into salvation, eternal life, and Covenant, and the unseen realities of God's Kingdom begin to be realized in us. These realities are inseparable.

Who is the King who reigns in the Kingdom of Heaven, and what is the Kingdom's eternal meaning to those who believe in Him? Foremost, why is this Kingdom not our object of focus? The announcement of the birth of God's Son to Mary came with the understanding of His mission to bring about the Kingdom of Heaven in the hearts of men. Notice in what follows that He will have the throne of His ancestor David, reigning forever, and His Kingdom has no end. Even His name, although it was one of the most common names in His day, was pregnant with meaning to a Jew. The Messiah's name is understood on the basis of who He is and what he will do! The "Tetragammatron," the four sacred letters of God's name, is *YHVH* (or *YHWH*). The letters in Hebrew are *Yud, Heh, Vav, Heh.* Jesus' Hebrew name "Yeshua," which is a contraction of the Hebrew name "*Y'hoshua*" (English Joshua), and means YHVH saves, is also the masculine form of the Hebrew word *Yeshua'ah*, which means salvation.

When we understand that Jesus' name in Hebrew is *Yeshua* and means "The LORD saves," we can also understand that as the Son of God, Jesus is *YHVH Yeshuati*—The LORD our Salvation. The Divine Name is found in many portions of Scripture. *YHVH Yeshuati,* "the LORD our salvation, or *Elohim Yeshuati,* God our Salvation, is One.[1] He is *Emmanu'El,* God with us. Jesus is *YHVH* our *Yeshuati,* Salvation; *YHVH Tzidkenu,* the LORD who causes me to be righteousness; and with this wonderful gift of righteousness, and wholeness: *YHVH Shalom,* the LORD our Peace. He is YHVH Mekadesh: the Lord who causes me to be holy, our Sanctifier. Paul sums this understanding in his letter to the Corinth church. This verse sums up salvation: "But by His doing you are in Christ Jesus, who

---

[1] Dr. Roy Blizzard contributed greatly to my understanding of salvation from a Jewish perspective. His influence in developing my understanding of Jesus' name and the salvation He brought was invaluable in grasping the vital concepts of salvation, righteousness and wholeness. Dr. Blizzard's material can be found at www.biblescholars.org.

became to us wisdom from God, and righteousness and sanctification, and redemption" (1Cor. 1:30). The angel said to Mary:

> And behold, you will conceive in your womb, and bear a son, and you shall name Him Jesus. He will be great, and will be called the Son of the Most High; and the Lord God will give Him the throne of His father David; and He will reign over the house of Jacob forever; and His kingdom will have no end. (Luke 1:31-33)

Many promises foretold the Kingdom and the King's coming. Luke hints back to one such important verse in Isaiah:

> For a child will be born to us, a son will be given to us; and the government will rest on His shoulders; and His name will be called Wonderful Counselor, Mighty God, Eternal Father, Prince of Peace. There will be no end to the increase of His government or of peace, on the throne of David and over his kingdom, to establish it and to uphold it with justice and righteousness from then on and forevermore. (Isaiah 9:6-7)

A child may be born, but a Son is given, and His kingdom is the Eternal Kingdom. In these verses, Isaiah is taking us back even to Genesis, to Jacob's prophecy to the tribe of Judah, from which the Lord descended—He is the lion of Judah (Rev 5:5):

> The scepter shall not depart from Judah, nor the ruler's staff from between his feet, until Shiloh comes, and to him shall be the obedience of the peoples. (Gen 49:10)

This great King, the mighty God, the Prince of peace, shall reign forever, and He shall forge obedience in the hearts of His people. "Shiloh" is often referred to as the "gathering." It is a Messianic term indicating the Kingdom this King oversees shall have a gathering to Him in the last days. Daniel also speaks of this eternal dominion:

> I kept looking in the night visions, and behold, with the clouds of heaven One like a Son of Man was coming, And He came up to the Ancient of Days and was presented before Him. And to Him was given dominion, glory and a kingdom, that all the peoples, nations, and men of every language might serve Him. His dominion is an everlasting dominion, which will not pass away; and His kingdom is one which will not be destroyed. (Dan. 7:13)

The Kingdom of God (and the Kingdom of "Heaven," which again is a euphemism for "God") is not a place or unified state such as Israel had under its kings. The Kingdom of God consists of (1) the King, (2) the realm of His rule, (3) the people of the King, and (4) the divine force at work within the Kingdom. Thus, the Kingdom includes those who come into the Kingdom's redemptive forward movement of Jesus Christ to bring God's Rule (His absolute rule) to earth by becoming His disciples—obeying His commands and teachings, and continuing His Kingdom work—taking His yoke. The Kingdom of Heaven is a spiritual realm, and God exists in this unseen realm. The Kingdom of Heaven is the present reality of a future inheritance.

To reiterate, to be under God's rule or reign means to obey God, to walk in His ways and thus fulfill His purpose. The Divine force in the Kingdom is God's power at work to bring His redemptive purpose to pass in the earth—His saving and healing power. Thus the Kingdom is redemptive in nature. It is a spiritual realm, a dimension, but the unseen realities of this spiritual Kingdom manifests in salvation, which is righteousness, healing, deliverance, wholeness and peace (Luke 11:20). The spiritual "unseen realities" actually govern the physical. When we learn of this spiritual dimension, we can begin to operate in its principles.

Concisely, God's rule over His people, His realm or dimension, the people under His rulership, and the manifestation of His power that brings salvation in its complete aspects, all constitute the Kingdom. The Kingdom is both within those who believe in God's Son (Luke 17:21), who brought the Kingdom into personal manifestation, and in the future complete manifestation of the kingdom in the millennium and beyond. The Kingdom is therefore at the same time both a spiritual reality that is fulfilled in individuals in the Kingdom, and a reality about to be fulfilled in the future. It is as George E. Ladd coined it, "the presence of the future." However, the manifestation of each age is unique.

The principal of the Kingdom is complete obedience to God—to the commands of the King (a democracy is foreign to kingdom living). Jesus' teachings focused on the Kingdom and the characteristics of those in the Kingdom. **Love is the foremost example of Kingdom living** (see Chapter Six).

When Jesus taught, He spoke not only of this age, but that age to come. It is a time when we shall see Him fully. The redemptive nature of the Kingdom is revealed in the purpose the Lord states for His coming. Remember, the Lord Jesus often spoke and acted as God, who says in Ezekiel:

> For thus says the Lord GOD, "Behold, I Myself will search for My sheep and seek them out. I will seek the lost, bring back the scattered, bind up the broken, and strengthen the sick; but the fat and the strong I will destroy. I will feed them with judgment." (Ezek. 34:11, 16)

We can agree that God is speaking in this verse above. He says, "I myself will search for My sheep!" Jesus hints at His deity when He likewise says, "For the Son of Man has come to seek and to save that which was lost" (Luke 19:10). From Ezekiel we can see just who the lost are—those who are scattered, broken, and sick. These are in need of salvation (Blizzard "Luke 19:10"). [2] We have long missed the point. Salvation is at once separate from the world to come, yet at the same time, an entrance into it. When we experience the spiritual dimension, we have come into contact with unseen realities.

---

[2] Dr. Roy Blizzard contributed greatly to my understanding of salvation from a Jewish perspective. His influence in developing my understanding of Jesus' name and the salvation He brought was invaluable in grasping the vital concepts of salvation, righteousness and wholeness. Dr. Blizzard's material can be found at www.biblescholars.org.

Messengers of Peace

We can confidently say that God intends for His people to experience absolute wholeness in the Kingdom. The sick, broken, lost and scattered, He wants to heal and bring into the Kingdom. Laborers for the Harvest need to be equipped with the same purpose. The biblical record tells us that Jesus sent His disciples to preach the kingdom, heal the sick, raise the dead, and cast out demons:

> And He called the twelve together, and gave them power and authority over all the demons, and to heal diseases. And He sent them out to **proclaim the kingdom of God**, and to perform healing. (Luke 9:1-2)

He accepted no excuses: "Allow the dead to bury their own dead; but as for you, go and **proclaim everywhere the kingdom of God!**" (Luke 9:60). This is a part of the great commission for any who would follow the Lord: Proclaim the Kingdom. The sick need to be healed, the dead raised, and the demonized delivered.

Summary of the Kingdom:
1. The concept of the kingdom of God is crucial to understanding the Bible. It refers to neither a place nor to a time, but to a condition in which God's rulership is acknowledged by humankind. It is a condition in which God's promises of a restored universe free from sin and death are beginning to be fulfilled (Jewish New Testament Commentary).

2. History can be divided into four periods: before Jesus, during his lifetime, the present age, and the future age. In a sense, the kingdom was present prior to Jesus birth, in that God was king over the Jewish people (1 Samuel 12:12).

3. Jesus' arrival brought a quantum leap in the earthly expression of the kingdom, for the fullness of all that God is was embodied in Him (Jewish New Testament Commentary: 1 Cor 2:9). We will see the full manifestation of the kingdom in the Millennium.

4. The Kingdom is the presence of the future. The kingdom of God comes immediately and truly but partially—to all who put their trust in Jesus and his message, thus committing themselves to live the holy lives God's rulership demands; for example, peace in the hearts even though there is not peace in the world is an example of partial yet full kingdom (Jewish New Testament Commentary).

5. The unseen realities of the Kingdom are made manifest in those who accept God's rule, enter the Kingdom, receive eternal life, the New Covenant, and an entrance into the age to come.

6. The Kingdom is the present reality of a future inheritance.

> *The unseen realities of the Kingdom are made manifest in those who accept God's rule, enter the Kingdom, receive eternal life, the New Covenant, and an entrance into the age to come.*

CHAPTER TWO

THE KINGDOM IS BREAKING FORTH AND ADVANCING

The Shepherd, the Stone of Israel

Jesus expected His followers to continue His Kingdom movement. They understood the forward movement of the Kingdom—it's advancing. The late Professor David Flusser of the Hebrew University explains the Kingdom in His book, <u>Jesus</u>. He discusses the realized eschatology of the Kingdom (the presence of the future kingdom), and explains that for Jesus and the rabbis, the Kingdom of God is both present and future, but their perspectives are different. According to Jesus, individuals are already in the Kingdom of Heaven. For Jesus, it was a **specific point in time when the kingdom began breaking out upon the earth.** "From the days of John the Baptist until now the Kingdom of Heaven is breaking through, and those who break through seize it" (Matt 11:12). "Every one forces his way in," according to Luke. Jesus words are based upon Micah (Flusser 110).

> I will indeed gather all of you, Jacob; I will collect the remnant of Israel. I will bring them together like sheep in a pen, like a flock in the middle of its fold. It will be noisy with people. One who breaks open *the way* will advance before them; they will break out, pass through the gate, and leave by it. Their King will pass through before them, the LORD as their leader. (Mic 2:12-13 HCSB)

This is a picture of those in the Kingdom breaking forth with their King. John the Baptist makes the breach, and the King/Shepherd goes forth with His flock leading them. They press through the breach and take possession of the Kingdom. We see a stampede to enter the Kingdom. The NIV translation characterizes this activity of breaking forth and advancing.

> From the days of John the Baptist until now, the kingdom of heaven has been forcefully advancing, and forceful men lay hold of it. For all the Prophets and the Law prophesied until John. And if you are willing to accept it, he is the Elijah who was to come (Matt. 11:12-14).

According to Flusser who quotes from J. Jeremias, Jesus is the only Jew of ancient times known to us who preached not only that people were on the threshold of the end of time, but that the new age of salvation had already begun. John the Baptist made the great breakthrough, but was not a member of the kingdom. The eruption of the Kingdom of God is an expansion among the people. "The Kingdom of Heaven is like leaven which a woman took and hid in three measures of meal, till all was leavened" (Matt. 13:33). "It is like a grain of mustard seed which a man took and sowed in his garden; and it grew and became a tree, and the birds of the air made nests in its branches" (Luke 13:18-19) (Flusser 110). The innate growth of the Kingdom means it spreads out as surely as a seed is programmed to produce; it happens unawares, but when ripe, harvested. Jesus compares:

> The Kingdom of God is as if a man should cast seed on the earth, and should sleep and rise night and day, and the seed should spring up and grow, he doesn't know how. (Mark 4:26-27) For the earth bears fruit: first the blade, then the ear, then the full grain in the ear. But when the fruit is ripe, immediately he puts forth the sickle, because the harvest has come. (Mark 4:28-29)

The Kingdom thus includes its people who are increasing greatly. The Kingdom of God is growing, and many are rushing into it, even the Gentiles. The birds making nests in the branches may illustrate the many nations who will come into the kingdom. Flusser notes:

For Jesus, the kingdom of heaven is not only the eschatological rule of God that has dawned already, but a divinely willed movement that spreads among people throughout the earth. The Kingdom of heaven is not simply a matter of God's kingship, but also the domain of his rule, an expanding realm embracing ever more and more people, a realm into which one may enter and find one's inheritance, a realm where there are both great and small. We do not mean to assert that Jesus wanted to found a church or even a single community, but he wanted to start a movement. Stated in exaggerated ecclesiological terms, we might say that the eruption of the Kingdom of Heaven is a process in which ultimately the invisible church becomes identical with the visible. (Flusser 110-111)

The One to come who brings the Kingdom realm, and the eschatological refiner and Judge that Israel looked forward to is One person. He is *YHVH Yeshua*, the Lord our Salvation. He will bring salvation, and He will bring recompense, justice for both the least and the greatest. John the Baptist did not understand, as did many others, that Jesus would first make salvation real, then at God's appointed time at the end of days, He would appear again as the Son of Man in great glory. John the Baptist makes the great breakthrough and he is the messenger who goes before YHVH to prepare a way. He goes before the "messenger of the covenant" who comes suddenly to His Temple. He brings the New Covenant and manifests the Kingdom. Malachi prophesies:

> "Behold, I am going to send My messenger, and he will clear the way before Me. And the Lord, whom you seek, will suddenly come to His temple; and the **messenger of the covenant**, in whom you delight, behold, He is coming," says the LORD of hosts. "But who can endure the day of His coming? And who can stand when He appears? For He is like a refiner's fire and like fullers' soap. And He will sit as a smelter and purifier of silver, and He will purify the sons of Levi

and refine them like gold and silver, so that they may present to the LORD offerings in righteousness. Then the offering of Judah and Jerusalem will be pleasing to the LORD, as in the days of old and as in former years. Then I will draw near to you for **judgment**; and I will be a swift witness against the sorcerers and against the adulterers and against those who swear falsely, and against those who oppress the wage earner in his wages, the widow and the orphan, and those who turn aside the alien, and do not fear Me," says the LORD of hosts. "For I, the LORD, do not change; therefore you, O sons of Jacob, are not consumed." (Mal. 3:1-6 Emphasis added)

Jesus quotes from these verses, and He shows the connection that the people of His day would have grasped. Those who heard John's message and received John's baptism were typically the despised of his day, the tax collectors, outcasts, and sinners. Those who are the least in the eyes of most become greater than John, having received "God's justice" and entered the Kingdom through the "messenger of the covenant," the Lord Himself, YHVH Yeshua. Yet the Pharisees and scribes did not receive John's baptism and a receptive heart, thereby rejecting God's purpose for it. If one accepted what John proclaimed, "repent and be baptized," it produced a person receptive to the Lord's coming with Covenant blessings of salvation. Jesus says:

> "But what did you go out to see? A prophet? Yes, I say to you, and one who is more than a prophet. This is the one about whom it is written, 'Behold, I send My messenger before Your face, Who will prepare Your way before You.' I say to you, among those born of women, there is no one greater than John; yet he who is **least in the kingdom of God is greater** than he." And when all the people and the tax-gatherers heard this, **they acknowledged God's justice**, having been baptized with the baptism of John. But the Pharisees and the lawyers rejected God's purpose for themselves, not having been baptized by John. (Luke 7:26-30)

The least in the kingdom is greater than John, the one who made the breakthrough, but who did not enter into it. John fulfilled his purpose to proclaim the Lord's coming, but He looked for the Son of Man in the eschatological sense, which will happen at the end of days. The One who would "baptize with the Holy Spirit and with fire" is yes, at the same time, One person, but the two aspects of His mission are in separate ages. He came with salvation, justice, and the Holy Spirit to those who would repent and receive Him, and He will come again with recompense, and "who can stand at His coming."

While Jesus preached, "Repent, the Kingdom of God is at hand," He was speaking of the present reality of salvation available to those who would accept His claim and come into the Kingdom. He declares in His teachings and parables that He is the eschatological Son of Man, the one who would separate the goats and sheep at the end of days, but unlike John the Baptist and Jews of His days, Jesus points to a future time of its total fulfillment. The kingdom has come, but partially. The threshold of the end of the age comes into sight at the Lord's coming, and with it salvation. Those alive after the Lord's ascension stood at the threshold and looked for the door to open to the new age, and we alive today, still look. It is opening, but until that time, the "blessed hope" of His appearing is burning in us.

THE KINGDOM IS POWER

The reality of the Kingdom is present in Jesus' miracles and message of Kingdom salvation. He shows that He is the Son of Man in the sense of the long awaited Messiah, but He would first make the Kingdom real by the authority and power He exercises over His enemies. He brings the spiritual dimension of God's authority into the natural. When He performs healings, miracles, or raises the dead, He is bringing God's Kingdom into manifestation. If we can but accept the unseen realities of God's Kingdom, we can begin to understand the power of this Kingdom.

When Jesus binds the "strong man," strips him of his armor, and robs him of his power, the Kingdom is made manifest. Satan is rendered powerless.

> But if I cast out demons with the finger of God, surely the kingdom of God has come upon you. When a strong man, fully armed, guards his own palace, his goods are in peace. But when a stronger than he comes upon him and overcomes him, he takes from him all his armor in which he trusted, and divides his spoils. He who is not with Me is against Me, and he who does not gather with Me scatters. (Luke 11:20-23)

Jesus says the Kingdom has burst forth "upon you." He demonstrates authority and power to cast out demons, heal diseases and raise the dead. Obviously, those who are demonized or oppressed by the devil with sickness come out from under Satan's power when the Kingdom breaks upon them—God is in charge! Just as when God led the Israelites out of Egypt and defeated their enemies at the Red Sea, and they saw the Kingdom (His power to save and deliver), Jesus reveals the Kingdom and delivers those oppressed by Satan (demonstrates its power), by overthrowing Satan. "Upon the Red Sea, Israel first sang the praise of God's Kingdom (Ex. R. and Targ. Yer. to Ex. xv. 19) (Jewish Encyclopedia).

Jesus Christ exercised authority and power over Satan and delegated this same authority and power to those who are in union with Him; however, Satan continues to attempt to oppress those whom he can. We know that one day, he will be bound for a season during the Millennium, and subsequently cast into the lake of fire. Until then, the Kingdom of God and His Christ must be proclaimed. Paul says, "For He must reign until He has put all His enemies under His feet" (1Cor. 15:25). This last enemy is death. Through Christ's resurrection and our union with Him, we are delivered from fear of death, but death remains an enemy (Heb 2:14). Thus, the kingdom has broken forth, the age of salvation revealed, and the powers of the age to come made available, but full manifestation of the kingdom is awaiting this last enemy's defeat.

Deliverance, healing, safety, prosperity and fullness of the Spirit are a part of Covenant and Kingdom reality. Salvation is more than an entrance into the world to come; it is freedom and life in this age of the Kingdom. Salvation is an expression of the spiritual dimension that is present in God's Kingdom. Many who came to

Jesus were not looking for eternal life; they wanted healing, which is salvation for this age. Jesus sent His disciples out and they returned with joy after experiencing the power of the Kingdom:

> Then the seventy returned with joy, saying, "Lord, even the demons are subject to us in Your name." And He said to them, "I saw Satan fall like lightning from heaven. Behold, I give you the authority to trample on serpents and scorpions, and over all the power of the enemy, and nothing shall by any means hurt you. Nevertheless do not rejoice in this, that the spirits are subject to you, but rather rejoice because your names are written in heaven." (Luke 10:17-20)

Demons are subject to the authority of the Kingdom. Air is considered the realm where demons dwell, but they work in the hearts of men to influence for evil. Satan, whom Paul describes as "the prince of the power of the air" is subject to the King, and we are in Him (Eph 2:2). That puts us over any demonic power in the spiritual realm. Paul says that we bump up against these things, so we must put on the full armor of God and stand against them (Eph 6:12-13). You see the Kingdom when you see His power manifested in healing, deliverance, removal of yokes, and unclean spirits cast out: "But I say to you truthfully, there are some of those standing here who shall not taste death until they see the kingdom of God" (Luke 9:27).

God wants us to experience this dimension, the unseen realities of His Kingdom. He gave us His Spirit. God's Spirit is our conductor, the connection into a deeper dimension of the Spiritual realm. In union with our spirit, God's Spirit (He is also the pledge or guarantee of our inheritance) is at once both a sure sign of the Kingdom and its unseen realities, and the way we experience God's power in our lives.

Prayer Releases Power

Prayer is the principle conduit that brings us into contact with the spiritual forces in this unseen realm. The fruit of prayer is real revelation. It makes God's redemptive work effective in our age, as does using our delegated position of authority over certain areas of this dimension. Preaching and teaching the Kingdom of Heaven allows the Holy Spirit to bring conviction, but each must respond to God's invitation. The good news of Christ and His Kingdom is the power of God unto salvation (Romans 1:16).

The unseen realities of this Kingdom are thus greatly influenced by our prayer life. Jesus' prayer life and His authority over this spiritual dimension is our example of how we can best fulfill God's purposes on earth. James writes, "The earnest (heartfelt, continued) prayer of a righteous man makes tremendous power available [dynamic in its working]" (James 5:15b AMP). Prayer releases power. Some day perhaps we will see what affect our prayers had in the battle of the forces in this realm—for we know that God's armies (He is the Lord of Hosts) wage a mighty warfare against those forces who fight for supremacy against us.

> *Prayer is the principle conduit that brings us into contact with the spiritual forces in this unseen realm.*

Jesus was among very few who historically called God "Abba" (Father) in prayer. His intimacy with God is a trait shared by other holy men shortly before and after Him who worked miracles. It is a sense of sonship that those who spend time with Him understand and enjoy. Writes Flusser:

> The miracle worker is closer to God than other men. Jesus distinguishes between God as the common father of the believer, and God as *his* Father. . .the church's Christology includes an understanding that Christ has given to the believer the Spirit of His sonship (Romans 8:15) (Flusser 113, 118).

The big difference between those who worked miracles and were esteemed as holy men with intimacy with God: they prayed for miracles and received from God, but Jesus often commanded miracles, another proof He is the Christ.

Prayer is about intimacy with God. He gives answers to us in prayer, divine grants that may come to us as miracles. God establishing us as His holy people, set apart for Him for eternity, and giving us His Spirit as the pledge of our inheritance, puts us in a league with Jesus, joint heirs of the Kingdom of Heaven.

The Witnessing Body

Jesus wanted God's Kingdom to move forward through a witnessing body of believers, what we call the church. For the first few years, this movement was only through Jewish believers who remained a part of the Jewish faith, complying with its laws and ordinances. As more and more Gentiles came into the witnessing community, and persecution followed, Gentile believers in Jesus and His Kingdom message outnumbered the Jewish believers (this body of Jewish believers is identifiable into the third century). The Gentile witnessing body, spearheaded by a Jewish Rabbi named Saul (Paul to the Gentiles) advances even more rapidly than among the Jewish faithful. The mustard seed picture of the kingdom expands into a huge and growing tree where the nations build nests (Luke 13:19).

CHAPTER THREE

THE FIRST KINGDOM

God created human beings from His own nature, godlike, a reflection of His own Being.

God wants to give us a picture of the Kingdom. So when Jesus says, "But seek for His kingdom, and these things shall be added to you. Do not be afraid, little flock, for your Father has chosen gladly **to give you the kingdom**" (Luke 12:31-32 Emphasis added), we need to ask, how do you give something like a kingdom. God is King. Does that mean we inherit a domain where we reign as kings? And if He gives the Kingdom, is it:

> *God put Adam and Eve in a Kingdom paradise, and He gave them provision, power, purpose, protection, and best of all, His Presence.*

1. Something material and transferable?
2. A realm or domain in which we reign?
3. Limited in scope?
4. What exactly is our part, and what is God's part in its manifestation?

Jesus' teachings on the Kingdom bring to mind God giving us exactly what He intended for His first man to enjoy. Think about man's first domain. God put Adam and Eve in a Kingdom paradise, and He gave them provision, power, purpose, protection, and best of all, God's Presence. Eden's Kingdom, a paradise, consisted of everything to sustain life—thus provision. Adam and Eve could eat of every tree in the garden except one, so they had freedom within limits, an aspect of dominion.

Man's dominion consisted of power—he ruled over every created thing, but not people. One of the first Keys of Kingdom living: God, the King, appoints man his deputy authority, a viceroy, whom He puts in charge of a domain, an area or realm of delegated authority. A viceroy is like a governor who represents a sovereign or country. We see a picture of this in Joseph, whom Pharaoh put in command over all Egypt, and Daniel, of whom it is written that two successive kings made him viceroy over a great territory—their domain. God crowns man to be His viceroy, a king in his own right. But the king is subject to God, who is King of Kings. Great kings of the past in Babylon, such Artaxerxes and Nebuchadnezzar, enjoyed this title, but Paul ascribes it to God: "He who is the blessed and only Sovereign, the King of kings and Lord of lords" (1Tim. 6:15). This same title is bestowed upon our Lord Jesus in Revelations. If He is King of Kings, and Lord of Lords, and God seated us with Him as joint heirs, then we may also take the title of viceroy, and even more, king and lord (Ephes 2:6, Rev. 17:14, Rev. 19:16).

> *One of the Keys of Kingdom living: God, the King, appoints man his deputy authority, a viceroy, whom He puts man in charge of a domain, an area or realm of delegated authority.*

Gladly we honor Him as King of Kings and Lord of Lords, and we can look to one another as fellow heirs, fellow kings and lords to our God. As kings, we reign in life through Christ over our domains—our businesses or area of wealth, and as lords, we exercise our power to influence others for the Kingdom. It is a righteous way of living, a powerful way of living, which causes others to desire to enter the Kingdom.

God gave man a purpose as well. God told his man to cultivate the garden and thus care for his realm of dominion. In this protected environment, harmony existed between man and his surroundings. Without discord, man enjoyed God's protection. Thus in God's Kingdom, man had a great sense of security and significance. Genesis tells us that God walked with His man in the cool of the evening. Man enjoyed God's Presence.

> *Without discord, man enjoyed God's protection. Thus in s God's Kingdom, man had a great sense of security.*

God's Presence brought the spiritual reality of His Kingdom into the natural. Man enjoyed a spiritual dimension that merged with the physical. The spiritual dimension governs the physical dimension.

When man decided freedom within limits and being under God's rulership was secondary to his desires, it caused a traumatic event in creation. Sin brought disharmony in every area of this

Kingdom and ultimately death, something foreign to God's original design. God expelled man from Eden, and with the expulsion man lost his sense of provision, power, purpose, protection, and God's Presence. Man lost his sense of security and value. Man forfeited his idyllic kingdom until Jesus, the second Adam, bought it back.

Take note of how important it is to understand the Kingdom. Our King provides all! He wants His people to live in security—His protection, to have a purpose, to enjoy provision, a privileged relationship, and the power of dominion.

When Jesus came, His purpose was to restore the Kingdom to mankind. He wanted to rekindle man's relationship with His Creator, to release him from bondage and give him dominion. Lastly, to provide the kind of relationship that assures provision, power, purpose, protection, and Presence.

Consequently, when Jesus says, "Be anxious for nothing," "Stop worrying," and "seek His Kingdom," He is giving a kingdom principle. In the Kingdom, God's man enjoys a royal and privileged position of sonship. He is not merely a subject but a member of God's family. Typically in a monarchy, the King or Queen is usually very wealthy, and while he or she may provide certain amenities for his or her people, in most cases, the rich get richer, and the poor get poorer because of taxes, forced labor, or poor rulership. This is not so in God's Kingdom!

> *Typically in a monarchy, the King or Queen is usually very wealthy, and while he or she may provide certain amenities for his people, in most cases, the rich get richer, and the poor get poorer. This is not so in God's Kingdom!*

A short history lesson shows us that God intended for His people to remain a theocracy with Him as their only king, but they wanted to have an earthly king like other nations. It displeases God greatly, and He tells Samuel what the outcome will be:

> Listen to the voice of the people in regard to all that they say to you, for they have not rejected you, but they have rejected Me from being king over them (1 Sam 8:7 11). And he said, "This will be the procedure of the king who will reign over you: he will take your sons

and place them for himself in his chariots and among his horsemen and they will run before his chariots. And he will appoint for himself commanders of thousands and of fifties, and some to do his plowing and to reap his harvest and to make his weapons of war and equipment for his chariots. He will also take your daughters for perfumers and cooks and bakers. And he will take the best of your fields and your vineyards and your olive groves, and give them to his servants. And he will take a tenth of your seed and of your vineyards, and give to his officers and to his servants. He will also take your male servants and your female servants and your best young men and your donkeys, and use them for his work. He will take a tenth of your flocks, and you yourselves will become his servants. Then you will cry out in that day because of your king whom you have chosen for yourselves, but the LORD will not answer you in that day." (1 Sam 8:11-15)

From God's Kingdom perspective, earthly kingdoms are upside down, even one with what is considered a "good king." The Heavenly King instead makes His subjects His primary object for bestowing gifts. We do not make Him rich; He already owns it all. He takes care of us! Jesus wants us to know that our King, if we will enjoy our freedom within limits—just what He gave Adam, will provide for every need. It is His delight. God is the quintessential philanthropist, the pattern for all giving. He is a good King, and living in a theocracy is a blessing instead of a burden. This freedom within limits means we are under God's rule, and we obey His instructions. Having been restored to God in a special relationship, we enjoy a special sense of belonging, protection—a sense of security and value, and His Presence. He does not just walk with us in the evening, but He is in us and with us! Listen to the Message translation—it captures the essence of Jesus' words:

> What I'm trying to do here is get you to relax, not be so preoccupied with *getting* so you can respond to God's *giving*. People who don't know God and the way he

works fuss over these things, but you know both God and how he works. Steep yourself in God-reality, God-initiative, God-provisions. You'll find all your everyday human concerns will be met. Don't be afraid of missing out. You're my dearest friends! The Father wants to give you the very kingdom itself. (Luke 12:29-32 MSG)

God's Royal Ambassadors

With such good news, how can we not become God's royal Kingdom ambassadors? Jesus sent His disciples out with a command to make disciples—the highest possible calling. Paul preached the good news of the Kingdom and described himself as an ambassador: "Therefore, we are ambassadors for Christ, as though God were entreating through us; we beg you on behalf of Christ, be reconciled to God" (2 Cor 5:20).

God operates under this concept of "agency." We are His agents to others. We have authority to speak on His behalf. This is our royal message of the Kingdom: "God was in Christ reconciling the world to Himself, not counting their trespasses against them, and He has committed to us the word of reconciliation" (2 Cor 5:19). An agent or ambassador represents his King or nation—he speaks for him. When he takes his message to those in a foreign country, he may speak about his king's desire for peaceful relations. An ambassador may also claim diplomatic immunity on foreign soil—a picture of our authority and freedom from the devil's wiles and condemnation. While we are sojourners on this earth and must do business in the world's systems, it is much as though we are in a foreign country, and must claim our privileges.

An ambassador must represent the king in his dress and actions. Since he speaks for the king or president, he must say what the king would say, and overall, act like royalty. Even though the ambassador's home is in his own nation, while in a foreign country, the land on which he lives is his domain and owned by his home nation. He has dominion over it. As God's royal viceroys, kings and deputy authorities, we are also priests unto Him, ministering to Him from our heart. Peter calls us a royal priesthood:

> But you are a chosen race, a royal priesthood, a holy nation, a people for God's own possession, that you may proclaim the excellencies of Him who has called you out of darkness into His marvelous light. (1Pet. 2:9)

THE PRINCIPLE OF GOD'S PRESENCE AND SOVEREIGNTY

The Presence of God in and with every man in the Kingdom insures man does not go unchecked as man rules as God's viceroy, king, or lord. Whatever the title we ascribe to our reign in life, were it not for the indwelling Presence, the Holy Spirit in us and upon us, we would not enjoy the anointing and grace to fulfill our purpose in life. We would be led astray.

If one looks at some earthly kingdoms, those who have rejected God's direct rule, they are in darkness. God is Sovereign, but some have tried to take over—usurping God's rightful place of authority. Only by His grace can we avoid the corruption in the world. King Nebuchadnezzar is an example of one who tried; He had to eat grass! Daniel writes:

> How are you fallen from heaven, O Shining One, son of Dawn! How are you felled to earth, O vanquisher of nations! "For you have said in your heart: I will ascend into heaven, I will exalt my throne above the stars of God; I will also sit on the mount of the congregation, on the farthest sides of the north." (Isa14:12-13)

The "stars of God" is a term referring to the Israelites. Scholars agree that the body of verses in Isaiah 14, which many apply to Satan, refers to King Nebuchadnezzar. What some ascribe to Satan, some translations say Lucifer, is about this king who became prideful. Satan is not a light bringer! "Lucifer" should be translated "howl." Adam Clarke translates: "Howl, son of the morning; I will get the empire of the whole world. I will exalt my throne above the stars of God-above the Israelites, who are here termed the stars of God. So the Targum of

Jonathan, and R." (Clarke). God judges this King, and Daniel delivers the message of God's sovereignty:

> And they shall drive you from men, and your dwelling shall be with the beasts of the field. They shall make you eat grass like oxen; and seven times shall pass over you, until you know that the Most High rules in the kingdom of men, and gives it to whomever He chooses. (Dan. 4:32)

Can we not see that God is sovereign and that He involves himself in mankind's kingdoms? Also, we must not allow what we have heard others repeat about the biblical text decide for us; rather, study and like the Berean's act more nobly by examining the scriptures, and in some cases, the wealth of biblical Hebrew commentaries (Acts 17:11).

Satan, who attempts to influence men through their minds, will attempt to deceive and lead us astray, just as he tried to do with Jesus, but we have the Holy Spirit to help us. When Satan tempted the Lord Jesus, I am sure it was the same way he tempts us, through His mind. For some uncanny reason, Satan has the power to give us thoughts that are ungodly and unrighteous. When he tempted Jesus in the wilderness at the end of Jesus' fast, he came with an attack aimed at getting Jesus to deny God's authority and kingdom. Satan wanted Him to both test God and worship Satan—a violation of a worship commandment and a commandment of the Torah in Deuteronomy.

The attack on the Lord's mind included a vision of all the kingdoms of the world that Satan claimed to own. Satan's temptation appealed to Jesus' mission; would Jesus take God's way of establishing the Kingdom or disobey and worship Satan, which was anathema to a devout Jew like Jesus? Satan says, "_Since_ you are the Son of God, command these stones to become bread." "Since" can also be translated as "If." This is like saying, "_Since_ you are Deity, command these stones to be bread." In a subsequent temptation, Jesus responds, "It is said, 'You shall not put the Lord your God to the test'" (Luke 4:12). Jesus' command of the Scriptures hints to something King Ahaz said, and to what Isaiah prophesied of the Messiah through Isaiah:

> "But Ahaz said, 'I will not ask, nor will I <u>test the LORD</u>!' Then he said, 'Listen now, O house of David! Is it too slight a thing for you to try the patience of men, that you will try the patience of my God as well? Therefore the Lord Himself will give you a sign: Behold, a virgin will be with child and bear a son, and she will call His name Immanuel.'" (Isa 7:12-14)

Jesus is too smart for Satan. Not only did Jesus overcome, but also He left us some strong hints at His name, Immanu'El. Satan is a liar, and the father of lies. He cannot give kingdoms that belongs to God alone as Sovereign. He wanted Jesus to break Torah, and consequently make Him unfit as a spotless lamb. God provides our needs; we do not look to a usurper who wants to bring us under his darkness. Yes, Satan has a limited degree of authority, a kingdom of darkness to those who submit to sin, but not one that covers the whole world. God is in charge and will always reserve His Sovereign right over all. Jesus knew the voice of God. He knew Torah, the writings, the prophets, and the oral law. We must do the same if we are to avoid deception, that is, know His word. The voice of God in His word is powerful, as is His indwelling Presence. Such Grace! Because Jesus overcame, we have our entrance into the eternal Kingdom, and the grace through the Holy Spirit to overcome sin.

The powers of the age to come that Jesus spoke of is also resident for us in the unseen realities of the Kingdom. For believers, having tasted of the Heavenly Gift, the Holy Spirit, and the powers of the age to come (see **Chapter Four** "Powers of the Age to Come"), a righteous way of living has emerged. In Paul's words, "for the Kingdom of God is not eating and drinking, but righteousness, shalom, and joy in the Holy Spirit" (Rom 14:17 HNV). We live in the present, but our feet are firmly planted also in the future.

Jesus said something remarkable to His disciples: "and just as My Father has granted Me a kingdom, I grant you that you may eat and drink at My table in My kingdom, and you will sit on thrones judging the twelve tribes of Israel" (Luke 29-30). This is a picture of the Kingdom in the age to come. Jesus intends for His disciples to reign with Him.

CHAPTER FOUR

THE AGE TO COME

*We live in the present, but our
feet are firmly planted in the future*

The Lord and the prophets before Him spoke of a future age marked by a universal cataclysmic event. In eschatological terms, they warned of the "Day of the Lord." While in captivity in Babylon, Daniel interprets a dream for the King that shows us the future for the Kingdom, how it shall prevail. God will set up a kingdom that will endure forever. A great stone cut without hands will crush the kingdoms of this world.

> And in the days of these kings shall the God of heaven set up a kingdom, which shall never be destroyed: and the kingdom shall not be left to other people, *but* it shall break in pieces and consume all these kingdoms, and it shall stand for ever. Forasmuch as thou sawest that the stone was cut out of the mountain without hands, and that it brake in pieces the iron, the brass, the clay, the silver, and the gold; the great God hath made known to the king what shall come to pass hereafter: and the dream *is* certain, and the interpretation thereof sure. (Daniel 2:44-45)

This is the mountain of God, and His Messiah's Kingdom is great and will reign over all others: "Who thou, O great mountain? Before Zerubbabel **upright**: and he shall bring forth the headstone shouting, 'Grace, grace unto it'" (Zech. 4:7, paraphrase). You may have heard or read this verse quoted as though we speak to a mountain to make it level. But the sages taught that the great mountain is Messiah, upright and just. The same word for plain or level also means upright or just. A rabbinic commentary says: "This is the King Messiah. And why is he called "a great mountain"? Because he is greater than the patriarchs— elevated beyond Abraham, exalted above

Moses and superior to the ministering angels" (Tanhuma, Toledot 134-138 [ed. Buber, 139]).

Jesus also spoke of the "age" to come when a future reward would be realized for those who fully followed Him. The "*olam haba*" is "the world to come." Sometimes the translators used "world" to come in lieu of the "age" to come. The Greek word for age is *aion*, which represents a period of time. The Greek word for world is *cosmos*, which represents something in social or orderly arrangement or proper order. It could be that translators have interchanged the two words on occasion incorrectly. For our purposes, we understand the age to come, the *olam haba*, is the future full manifestation of the Kingdom of Heaven, either on earth such as during the millennium or in Heaven. The point Jesus wants to make is more along the lines of experiencing the unseen realities of God's Kingdom, a portion of something in the present, that we can experience more completely in a future age. To the disciples He promised:

> And He said to them, Truly I say to you, There is no one who has left house, or parents, or brothers, or wife, or children for the sake of the kingdom of God, who shall not receive many times more in this **present time**, and, in **the world to come** everlasting life. (Luke 18:29-30 Emphasis added)

This age to come is what many look forward to as "Heaven." Jesus taught His disciples to pray, "Thy Kingdom come, Thy will be done, here on earth as it is in Heaven" (Luke 11:2). If His Kingdom is present in us and around us, then His will is being done! We have understood "in Heaven" to be a place instead of a dimension! The unseen realities of God's Kingdom are present. The spiritual dimension is present in the natural. We can see that what Jesus called "here on earth" is an age in which we now live. Someday, yes, we will see a new Heaven and a new Earth, but this will manifest in what He also called, "the age to come." Jesus is speaking of an age or a time when God's Kingdom will be fully realized. First we experience this age of kingdom living, the unseen realities even of the age to come, eternal life, New Covenant, salvation and a righteous way of living.

Then we enter the Millennium and ultimately, a new Heaven and a new Earth.

If Jesus said pray, "Thy Kingdom come," it must be possible to experience the Kingdom dimension and its unseen realities, which is also in part, the presence of the future age to come, now in this age. That means salvation for all who come under God's rule through Christ, covenant, eternal life, an entrance into the world to come, and as I frequently say, most of all, God's abiding Presence.

Jesus explained His purpose to seek and save the lost after the dramatic account of Zaccheus' turn around. Jesus announces that Salvation has come to Zaccheus' house (Luke 19:1-8). One who was lost has been found. "Salvation" to His disciples meant more than a place in the world to come, it meant healing, wholeness, safety, and a restoration of what was lost; i.e. restoration of the earthly Kingdom to its rightful owners.

The Lord knew that His disciples expected Him to ascend to the throne, and lead them out of Roman domination. While He told them that instead He was to be "handled over to the Gentiles" (Luke 18:33), their understanding was darkened. He tells them a parable that shows His Kingdom is still progressing; in fact, to the point that He will receive its fullness and return. God would arrange a glorious transfer of authority and dominion to His Son, whose Kingdom has no end.

> I saw in the night visions, and behold, One like the Son of man came with the clouds of heaven, and came to the Ancient of Days, and they brought Him near before Him. And dominion and glory was given Him, and a kingdom, that all peoples, nations and languages. (Daniel 7:13-14)

Rome's custom was to grant kingdoms or governments in the presence of the Emperor. Jesus' listeners would have recalled that Herod traveled to Rome to be appointed King and returned to Judea to reign. His parable in Luke 19 that follows points to His own heavenly reception and return, how His disciples should conduct themselves in His absence, and of judgment.

And as they heard these things, He added and spoke a parable, because He was near Jerusalem, and because they thought that the kingdom of God was about to appear immediately. Therefore He said, "A certain nobleman went into a far country to receive a kingdom for himself, and to return. And He called his ten servants and delivered ten minas, and said to them, Trade until I come back. But his citizens hated him. And they sent a message after him, saying, We will not have this one to reign over us. And when he had received his kingdom and had returned, then it happened that he commanded these servants to be called to him; the ones to whom he had given the silver; so that he might know what each had gained by trading. And came the first, saying, Lord, your mina has gained ten minas. And he said to him, Well done, good servant, because you have been faithful in a least thing, have authority over ten cities. And the second came, saying, Lord, your mina has made five minas. And he said the same to him, You be over five cities. And another came, saying, Lord, behold, here is your mina, which I have kept in a handkerchief. For I feared you, because you are a harsh man. You take up what you did not lay down, and you reap what you did not sow. And he said to him, I will judge you out of your own mouth, wicked servant! You knew that I was a harsh man, taking up what I had not laid down and reaping what I did not sow. And why did you not give my silver on the bank table, and coming I might have exacted it with interest? And he said to those who stood by, Take the mina from him and give it to him who has ten minas. And they said to him, Lord, he has ten minas. For I say to you that to everyone who has, more will be given. And from him who has not, even that which he has will be taken from him. But those who are my enemies, who did not desire that I should reign over them, bring them here and slay them before me." And saying these things, He went in front, going up to Jerusalem. (Luke 19:11-28)

The Lord wants His disciples to understand that the Kingdom has broken forth, and they are to occupy until He comes. This charge amounts to using the gifts and abilities that He gave us as stewards, because we will give an account in the Age to Come. If we cannot accept His yoke and reign in this life, and look to His coming, we cannot have it in the Age to Come.

When will He return and set up this powerful Kingdom fully? In the beginning, God established the seven-day week. The week is a prophetic type for the timing that God would use to work out His purpose for mankind. Just as seven days are in a week, God has a plan of 7,000 years for mankind. He gave six days to man to go about his own business, but the seventh day is God's time: a time when God's Kingdom will be fully established and His government will rule this whole earth. No other religion or government will exist on earth—only the reign of the Kingdom of God. We do not know the hour or day, but Jesus said, "This Good News of the Kingdom will be preached in the whole world for a testimony to all the nations, and then the end will come" (Matt 24:14 HNV). We have missed it by not fully preaching the Kingdom—it must go to all nations before the end comes.

THE POWERS OF THE AGE TO COME

A particular verse reverberates truth. It speaks of "tasting the powers of the age to come." The author of the letter to the Hebrews warns:

> For concerning those who were once enlightened and tasted of the heavenly gift, and were made partakers of the Holy Spirit, and tasted the good word of God, and **the powers of the age to come,** and then fell away, it is impossible to renew them again to repentance; seeing they crucify the Son of God for themselves again, and put him to open shame. (Heb 6:4-6 Emphasis added)

The late Kenneth E. Hagin functioned in the office of a prophet. As have other prophets in our day, Brother Hagin personally spoke with Jesus on a number of occasions. Either in an open vision or in some realm of the Spirit, Jesus appeared to him many times. Brother Hagin tells of one occasion when Jesus appeared to him and explained the above verses containing this phrase "powers of the age to come." Jesus explained the "enlightenment" as the conviction that brings one to see his need for a Savior. The "heavenly gift" that one may taste is Jesus Himself. He is the Heavenly Man that brings the indwelling presence of the Holy Spirit, and one is "born again." Actually one is "born from above" and makes a complete change of direction, turning to God. One could stop here, and many do. They never go beyond receiving new birth and the indwelling presence of the Holy Spirit. But obviously, Jesus' disciples, Jewish converts and Gentiles experienced more of the Holy Spirit, and we read about their experiences throughout the New Testament. They partook of Him. To be a "partaker of the Holy Spirit," Jesus explained, referred to baptism in the Holy Spirit (see Acts 1:5, 2:4). Further, "tasting the good word of God" involves enjoying the meat of the word of God, not just the milk of it, which the immature drink.

    Lastly, and the verse we need to look at closely, involves those who have "tasted the powers of the age to come." The present unseen realities of the Kingdom bring salvation, but the fullness of salvation, immortal bodies and much more come in the age to come. But in this life, one may "taste" powers of the age to come. The Lord told Brother Hagin, that tasting the powers of the age to come refers to mature Christians who have the "gifts of the Spirit" operating in their lives or ministries. He further explained that the baptism in the Holy Spirit with the ensuing gifts is the earnest of our inheritance in the world to come (Hagin 105-106).

    See what a great and wonderful gift the Lord poured out so graciously on us at Pentecost! Not only can we experience the indwelling presence of the Lord by the Holy Spirit at our conversion, and an entrance into the age to come, but also we can have more, the very ability of the Spirit He promised His disciples before He ascended (See Ephesians 1:13,14, 2 Cor 5:5, 1 Cor Chapters 12-14). This gift "opens the door" for spiritual gifts to flow.

The age to come is mentioned in many scriptures, and is often closely associated with Heaven. It is the Kingdom of God in full manifestation. Paul writes that God raised Christ "far above all rule, and authority, and power, and dominion, and every name that is named, not only in this age, but also in that **which is to come**" (Ephesians 1:21).

The age to come also includes the millennium in which Christ reigns over His Kingdom, and is followed by the Great White Throne Judgment, and the new heavens and new earth. This age will be marked by an enjoyment of God's Physical Presence. Revelations tells us that in that day, we have no need for a sun and moon, or a man-made temple. Christ Jesus is the lamp and the light is God Himself. This occurs in the heavenly Jerusalem, coming out of Heaven as a bride adorned for her groom.

> I saw no temple in it, for the Lord God, the Almighty, and the Lamb, are its temple. And the city has no need of the sun or of the moon to shine upon it, for the glory of God has illumined it, and its lamp is the Lamb. (Rev. 21:22-23)

> And I saw the holy city, new Jerusalem, coming down out of heaven from God, made ready as a bride adorned for her husband. (Rev. 21:2)

The Kingdom of God is also the Kingdom of His Dear Son. But in the last days, the age to come after the Millennium, Christ delivers the kingdom to God the Father. Paul gives revelation:

> Then comes the end, when He delivers up the kingdom to the God and Father, when He has abolished all rule and all authority and power. (1Cor. 15:24)

We know little about this age to come, both of the millennium and after, but only what scripture tells us of its everlasting peace and joy. We can experience a degree of it in the Kingdom in this age. Paul tells us about some of the unseen realities of God's Kingdom, "The

Kingdom of God is righteousness, peace and joy in the Holy Spirit" (Romans 14:7).

At the Lord's coming, we shall be "like Him." This means for us a glorified body, a position that includes power to reign with Christ, judging angels, and as judges, we are also deliverers. Most of all, we enjoy His Presence. We further know that all enemies of mankind will be subjected to Christ, including death, because death is an enemy, the last one to be destroyed. Paul says that Christ Jesus will reign until that time, "For He must reign until He has put all His enemies under His feet. The last enemy that will be abolished is death" (1 Cor 15:25-26). David prophesies of God's plan, "The LORD says to my Lord: Sit at My right hand, Until I make Thine enemies a footstool for Thy feet'" (Psalm 110:1). Once all the Son's enemies including death are subjected to Him, Christ will subject Himself to God. Paul exclaims, "And when all things are subjected to Him, then the Son Himself also will be subjected to the One who subjected all things to Him, that God may be all in all" (1 Cor. 15:28). To the praise of the glory of His grace!

The following diagram shows how all this fits together from the fall in the garden, to the covenants with Noah, Moses, and the New Covenant that brings the Holy Spirit at Pentecost. Notice that the Kingdom includes the powers of the age to come, present (dotted line) even before the catching away of the saints (the rapture/*parousia*). We see the present unseen realities of the Kingdom (adapted from *The Pauline Eschatology*).

The Threefold Manifestation of the Kingdom of God:

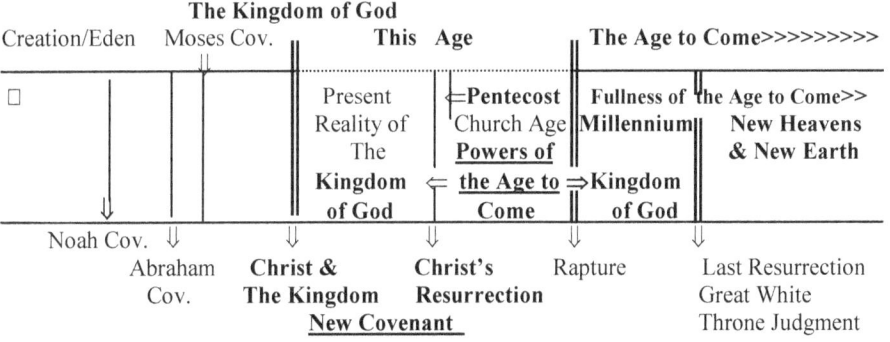

The threefold manifestation of the Kingdom is illustrated in the redemptive Kingdom coming in Jesus' ministry (yet not fully), the redemptive age of the church breaking forth at Pentecost endued with the powers of the age to come, and the age to come, which includes the millennium and beyond. The church experiences the redemptive Kingdom, and its unseen realities. It is empowered by the presence of the Holy Spirit and the possibility of enjoying the spiritual dimension. Lastly, it is endued with the powers of the age to come, and in the millennium ruling and reigning with Christ, and the new heavens and earth. We know that since He ascended, we shall likewise at His coming. Paul teaches: "But each in his own order: Christ the first fruits, after that those who are Christ's at His coming" (1Cor. 15:23).

Jesus said to Pilate, "My Kingdom is not of this world" (John 18:36a). The Complete Jewish Bible translates: My Kingdom does not derive it authority from the world's order of things" (John 18:36 CJB). The ordered world of Pilate and the Romans—their social and political sphere of authority, nearly covered the earth. Jesus talked of a Kingdom that superseded that of the natural order, not one that competed with it. The Kingdom has been called an invisible influence with a very visible result! His Kingdom produces those who would come under God's rule and submit to the authority of God, not resist it. When He is welcomed in hearts as King, His Kingdom comes. Even though Jesus commanded all authority in Heaven and in Earth, He submitted that authority to God's will and obeyed. Yes, we are to be like our Lord.

Historically, a shift occurred among Jewish followers of Jesus in understanding the expression of the Kingdom of Heaven. Jesus preached a Kingdom that was present in power and redemption. At the same time, it did not negate the future aspects of His Kingdom, to be known at His second coming and the age to come. He commanded His followers to love their enemies, thus warning against agitating Rome. Another Rabbi speaks of the events that followed:

> When, however, the trend of events led early Christianity to make a decided disavowal of all political expectations antagonistic to Rome, the conception of the Kingdom of God was made an entirely spiritual one, and was identified with the "'olam ha-ba" (= "the world

to come"), the spiritual life, in which "there is no eating and drinking, but righteousness and peace and joy in the holy spirit" (Rom. xiv. 17, Greek; comp. John xviii. 36). Rab speaks of it in the same way: "In the world to come there is neither eating, nor drinking, nor procreation, nor strife; but the righteous sit encrowned and enjoy the splendor of the Shekinah" (Ber. 17a). (Jewish Encyclopedia)

The righteous enjoy "ruling and reigning with Christ" in the age to come. Yet we are "seated with Him in the Heavenly places in Christ" right now, according to Paul. And we can enjoy in part the "splendor of Shekinah." The "Shekinah" is not a word in the Bible, but a biblical concept describing God's Presence in the writings of the sages. With the Presence of God's Spirit, we can both enter a dimension of His Spirit, the unseen realities of God's Kingdom and in prayer, encounter the unseen forces in this dimension (and in acts of kindness) that allow us to taste this future splendor.

The "powers of the age to come" are important, because through them, God uses us to help bring wholeness to His people and continue the works of Jesus. As in prayer and authority, where we can be vessels for God to bring His redemptive purpose into manifestation in earth, the body of Christ can experience wholeness also through these spiritual gifts of the "powers of the age to come." However, authority and Kingdom living is much broader in scope. True kingdom living is spiritual, and operates in a spiritual dimension, but it is manifested in obedience and righteous living, which encompasses more; that is, faith hope, and love, righteousness, joy and peace in the Holy Spirit.

CHAPTER FIVE

THE PRESENT AGE

Now abide faith, hope and love . . .

Jesus' message given to us in Matthew was first: "Repent for the Kingdom of God is at hand" (Matt. 3:2, 4:17,10:7; Mark 1:14). He proclaimed to Jews that they must turn from sin and to God because the Kingdom of God was at hand. To be "at hand" means the kingdom is not near or coming near but present. Jesus aligns His purpose in seeking the lost and healing the hurting to that of preaching the Kingdom. Luke records that the Lord said, "I must preach the kingdom of God to the other cities also, for I was sent for this purpose" (Luke 4:43). He then demonstrated by His ministry on earth that the Kingdom was present in power by casting out demons, healing the sick, raising the dead, and performing miracles.

> *The unseen realities of God's Kingdom, which includes the powers of the age to come, broke forth in the Person of Jesus Christ.*

The unseen realities of God's redemptive Kingdom, which includes the powers of the age to come, broke forth in the Person of Jesus Christ. He defeated the unseen enemies who cloaked themselves in sin and death. Jesus said it very clearly, "But if I cast out demons by the finger of God, then the kingdom of God has come upon you" (Luke 11:20). God is at work!

While His miracles manifested His glory and that of the Kingdom, the Lord refused to give signs to those who did not believe. He proclaimed, "The kingdom of God is not coming with signs to be observed; nor will they say, 'Look, here it is!' or, 'There it is!' For behold, the kingdom of God is in your midst" (Luke 17:20b-21). Still another translation says, "For behold, the kingdom of God is within you [in your hearts] *and* among you [surrounding you]" (Luke 17:21 AMP). Some have a problem with this understanding that the kingdom is within you, because Jesus is speaking to a group of Pharisees and scribes. Yet this group understood kingdom from the perspective of the sages. Jesus wants them to understand that the Kingdom of Heaven is present not only when God is ruling through their understanding of the yoke of Torah, but in His movement, which He invited them to join in bringing into fuller reality.

How can we have the Kingdom among us, within us, and surrounding us? We have to go to the definition of the Kingdom. For the Kingdom to be at work redemptively to accomplish God's purpose and continue the work the Lord Jesus gave His disciples, we must see the Kingdom not only as God's rule, and His realm, but also its people and its power, the divine force at work in the Kingdom. This spiritual dimension is made manifest when we accept God's Kingdom.

We have no power in and of ourselves. Yet Jesus said the "least in the kingdom is greater than John" (the Baptist), who Jesus described as having none who excelled him. Then we would ask, how is it possible for the least in God's Kingdom to be greater than John? The answer is the Kingdom within. We are united in one spirit with the King (1 Cor 6:17)! And we are endued with the Holy Spirit when we receive His abiding power (Acts 1:8). Foremost to us, we are accounted righteous by God through Christ's redemptive work. They can if they want to, but Gentile believers in Christ are not required to keep the 613 civil and religious laws of the Old Covenant to be set right with God, to draw near. The early apostles ruled on this matter in Acts 15. We can be justified by faith, and have peace with God through Christ (Romans 5:1).

> *We are united in one spirit with the King (1 Cor 6:17)!*

We are under the law of love, which fulfills all other commands. And God put His love in our hearts to enable us to fulfill this greatest of commands.

The Kingdom of Heaven has broken forth into the present age through Christ. God took us out of the darkness in which we were trapped. Through the same power that He used to raise Christ from the dead (Eph 1:20), God translated us out of darkness and into the Kingdom of His Son. We must give thanks—just as Paul encourages us:

> Giving thanks to the Father, who has qualified us to share in the inheritance of the saints in light. For He delivered us from the domain of darkness, and transferred us to the kingdom of His beloved Son. (Colossians 1:12-13)

The domain of darkness we have been delivered from is the realm in which the corruption of the world is at work. We have escaped it through Christ (2 Peter 1:4). We are saved from:
1. This perverse generation (Acts 2:40)
2. Corruption that is in the world (2 Peter 1:4)
3. From our wicked ways (Acts 3:26, Rev 18:4).
4. Judgment and condemnation (Acts 3:19)

Peter proclaims Jesus as the Messiah and the way of salvation to Israel: "No other name among men by which we must be **saved**" (Acts 4:12). Salvation means to be delivered, set free, secured, healed, made whole, and set right with God. By His grace, the free gift of righteousness comes as a result of repentance and receiving salvation.

THE GRACE OF THE KINGDOM

The present age is frequently called the "age of grace." However, grace is an ingredient of the Old and the New Covenants. In the era of the patriarchs, we find grace. But for grace, all of mankind would have been destroyed because of its wickedness; "But Noah found grace in the eyes of the Lord" (Gen 6:8). The Lord revealed His glory to Moses and described His goodness, "the Lord God, the Lord, **gracious,** compassionate, slow to anger, abounding in lovingkindness and truth, forgiving thousands of generations . . . (Gen 34). God does not change, and His attribute of graciousness is the same grace Jesus manifested. He was "full of grace and truth" (John 1:14,17). We forget that this age of grace is the age of the Kingdom of Heaven breaking forth and advancing.

The amazing grace of God is visible in His dealings with mankind. God reveals many pictures of the Kingdom in the Bible. The story of Joseph, which takes up the largest portion of the book of Genesis, is replete with types and shadows of Christ and the coming

Kingdom. Just a few of these types show us that Jacob shows favor toward Joseph, the son of Rachel, above his other sons, just as Christ was beloved of the Father and son of His love (Matt 3:17). As a teenager, Joseph has dreams of his brothers bowing down to him, even of his parents' homage. His brothers hate him because Joseph favored Jacob, and because of his seemingly presumptuous dreams—a picture of the prophecies by the Spirit of Christ through the Old Testament. Jacob makes Joseph a multicolored coat, the coat of the Kingdom.

> *Jacob makes Joseph a multicolored coat, the coat of the Kingdom.*

The brothers rip Joseph's coat apart and smear it with lamb's blood to deceive their father. We know the Sunday School stories of how his brothers betray Joseph and sell him into slavery in Egypt, and of how Joseph suffers, but is one day exalted to rule over Egypt, second only to Pharaoh. This is a picture of God's grace at work and of Christ's exaltation. The story's first ending shows Joseph and his brothers reconciled, and Joseph gives them a place to live in the best of Egypt, a land set apart from the rest of Egypt. Do you see another picture of the nature of the believer's life, set apart from the world?

The multicolored coat of the Kingdom indicated Joseph's royal favor; it was the dress of the heir and proof that Jacob treated Joseph as his eldest son. God gives us the robe of His favored, garments of salvation, the robe of righteousness (Isa 61:10). Outward clothing indicates what is on the inside. In the same way as Joseph was heir, Christ is heir of all things and we are joint heirs with Him in the Kingdom (Rom 8:17). If joint heirs with the King, then we are also royalty. We are to reign in this life with Him, and in the age to come, reign with Him "if indeed we suffer with Him in order that we may also be glorified with Him" (Rom 8:17). While tribulations and trials may come, we will overcome through Christ and be glorified with Him. In fact, our life is to be marked by grace's triumph as we reign through Him in this life, and enjoy our status as fellow heirs in the age to come. Grace is at work in our lives, as in the lives of those who preceded us, and grace is abundant. Writes Paul:

> *Our life is to be marked by grace's triumph as we reign through Him in this life, and in the age to come enjoy our status as fellow heirs.*

> For if by the transgression of the one, death reigned through the one, much more those who receive the abundance of grace and of the gift of righteousness will reign in life through the One, Jesus Christ. (Rom 5:17)

> But thanks be to God, Who in Christ always leads us in triumph [as trophies of Christ's victory] and through us spreads *and* makes evident the fragrance of the knowledge of God everywhere. (2 Cor 2:14 AMP)

THE KINGDOM FIRST

Too many of us are caught up in living the affluent life that we have in America. Our time is primarily spent in working to make a living instead of focusing on the eternal. God has placed eternity in our hearts (Eccl. 3:11), yet we are so busy with life, we forget our true focus. Jesus said the "cares of this life" and the "deceitfulness of riches" chokes the Word. On the other extreme, instead of filling our lives with things (when we finally learn they do not satisfy) some of us begin to search for something that will fill the void in us, bring fulfillment and wholeness, whether it is in a relationship or a job, or for some, freedom from self. We often begin to focus on life's barriers or obstacles to what is keeping us from advancing in freedom. If we begin to think, "If only we could have something, get over something, someone, our past, or be free of certain things or people," then these things will begin to be prominent; they will occupy our minds, hearts, and emotions. If we set our focus on the Lord, we will become more like Him:

> But we all, with unveiled face beholding as in a mirror the glory of the Lord, are being transformed into the same image from glory to glory, just as from the Lord, the Spirit. (2 Cor 3:18)

The principle is: what you behold, you will become. Our spirits are designed to bring into being what we behold, whether ugly or refined. We are continually becoming. As we focus on and therefore seek the Kingdom and God's righteousness, we will be changed.

Another way to make this point: you will both draw resources to and move toward your focus—you primary thought. What we forget is that what we are thinking about, and occupying ourselves with, we are likewise fellowshipping with! What we pay attention to we give power to—either transforming our lives for the better or worse. The significance we give to a person, an event, an action, or in the best possible way, God's Spirit, is the power it will have in our lives. Your energy and power become subservient to that which holds your focus. What holds your attention receives your power; it becomes a master to you and orders your existence. The answer to change is a change of focus, which will change your thinking. You act according to your thinking, and consistent actions lead to a change of behavior and ultimately, a change in your life. Is your focus on God and His Christ and Kingdom?

In the natural, what you focus your eyes on, you will move to. Policemen get run over because drivers focus on them and gravitate to them—as do runners. A vehicle crushed a friend of mine while running, because a driver must have started focusing on him, and the vehicle followed his eyes' focus.

What you focus on swallows your time, emotions, and transforms your existence; again, whether positive or negative. Oh that it would be the Kingdom of Heaven revealed in the Word of God! The very thing you wake up contemplating, perhaps spend your spare time thinking about or worrying about, your energy is attached to and you are drawn to it.

Jesus taught us to take no thought, so as to worry, about what we would wear or eat—life is more than food and drink and clothing. He says instead, "But seek for His kingdom, and these things shall be added to you. Do not be afraid, little flock, for your Father has chosen gladly to give you the kingdom" (Luke 12:31-32).

By now you see that what you put before you, and before all else, orders every issue of your life. Again, what you seek begins to mobilize and eventually order everything else in your life. This is true of good things and negative.

- Focus on television—it orders your life.
- Are you focusing on bondage—it orders your life.
- Are you focused on avoiding pain, or being rid of it—it will order your life and your finances in many cases.

In the same manner, seeking the kingdom will cause your life and issues of your life to be ordered around the Kingdom of God. It is true; we are transformed by renewing our minds (Romans 12:2).

We have ear gates, eye gates, and a heart gate (Prov 4:20). We are told to guard our hearts above all else for out of it flow the issues of life—the borders and boundaries, or in my words, the order of our life. You may gain knowledge of God, but for it to touch and transform your life so that you become the beautiful creature God intended, then God must be involved. Jesus said we could do nothing apart from Him. As someone said, "We need the Word and the Spirit—with the word only, we dry up, but with Spirit only, we blow up—we get flaky." We must not just gain knowledge, which puffs up (1 Cor 8:1), but we must experience it—we must have the action of the Holy Spirit at work in partnership with us. We must have His help.

The Principles of God and the Person of God bring freedom. Jesus said, "You will know the truth and the truth will set you free" (John 8:32)—no more seeking salvation by our efforts, but receiving resurrection power. God looses you to be who you should be the more you seek His Kingdom. Jesus says in John's gospel, "Abide in me, and my words abide in you" (John 15). Ingest the Person of God, and He begins to free you.

The Word and Spirit can transform how you see everything. We must therefore seek God's help. We must ask for His life and Kingdom to be paramount—the true knowledge of Him and His Son, Jesus Christ. If it is so crucial that we seek the Kingdom, then we must know for certain what is the Kingdom.

Jesus' teachings are filled with the characteristics of those in the kingdom and what the kingdom is like. He says to Nicodemus: "You cannot see the kingdom of God unless you are born from above" (John 3:3). To see (*ra'ah*) is to perceive, and expresses the idea of understanding and applying. The kingdom of Heaven is God's rule and realm, His people, the movement Jesus came to proclaim and advance, and its redemptive power. Everlasting life begins the minute new birth occurs, and we enter into God's House—where family lives. It is to be marked by the presence of God's glory. For the Spirit of God says, "the glory of the latter house shall be greater than the former," and believers are "Christ's House" (Heb 3:6), a glorious body of believers. "'The latter glory of this house will be greater than the former,' says the LORD of hosts, 'and in this place I shall give peace,' declares the LORD of hosts'" (Hag. 2:9).

While Jesus warned His disciples of His death, they did not understand. Jesus' teachings hinted strongly to the Old Testament, to the Son of Man, and the scriptures on the atonement, His death and resurrection, and by His faithfulness, the forgiveness of sins such as we now understand. But He taught boldly and forthrightly on the Kingdom and demonstrated the kingdom—its redemptive power.

THE VALUE OF THE KINGDOM OF HEAVEN

Jesus wanted His listeners and followers to understand the importance of seeking the Kingdom. He described its value in a number of parables designed to show the Kingdom's immeasurable worth. It is a treasure, worth selling all to purchase. It is a pearl of great price, so precious we should sell all to purchase it.

> The kingdom of heaven is like a treasure hidden in the field, which a man found and hid; and from joy over it he goes and sells all that he has, and buys that field. (Matt 13:43-44 MKJV).

> Again, the kingdom of heaven is like a merchant seeking fine pearls. (Matt. 13:47 MKJV)

When He talked about the culmination of the Kingdom, its final fulfillment to come, Jesus explained the Kingdom exists among and in the world. The people of the Kingdom of Heaven must live in the world along with those who are not of the Kingdom. While invisible, the unseen realities of the Kingdom are at work in its people. Jesus explains how those who are not of the Kingdom will be snatched out of it in the end times:

He presented another parable to them, saying, "The kingdom of heaven may be compared to a man who sowed good seed in his field. . . And in the time of harvest I will say to the reapers, 'First gather together the darnel and bind them in bundles to burn them, but gather the wheat into my granary.'" (Matt. 13:24-25 MKJV)

Again, the kingdom of heaven is like a dragnet cast into the sea, and gathering fish of every kind So it shall be at the end of the world. The angels shall come out and separate the wicked from among the just, and shall cast them into the furnace of fire. There shall be wailing and gnashing of teeth. (Matt 13:49-52 MKJV).

Count the Cost

With such value placed on the Kingdom, we can see that whatever the cost, those who understand its value will pay it gladly. To become a disciple of a Rabbi in Jesus' day meant that one had to leave home and family and travel with the Rabbi for a season. So important was study with the Rabbi that Jesus said one had to esteem it more than one's mother and father. This study had to consume the disciple's life and efforts, and the decision was one that had to be considered on the basis of cost.

Jesus said one must carefully consider a decision to follow Him. You cannot begin to follow in the footsteps of the Master and then change your mind—it shows you are not worthy of the Kingdom: "No one who puts his hand to the plow and looks back is fit for the kingdom of God" (Luke 9:62). The Lord gave parables about counting the cost. He tells of a man who decides to build a tower, and is ridiculed if he cannot finish it (Luke 14:28-33), and of a king going to war, and having to make peace instead (Luke 1:31-32). One had to leave all their possessions to follow a traveling Rabbi (Luke 14:33). Since Jesus was going about the villages and cities preaching the Kingdom—preaching, teaching and healing, He often endured exposure to the elements: "The Son of Man has no place to lay His head" (Luke 9:58).

To hate one's parents means to make them second in affection and to love something more, making it first in affection (Genesis 29:31). Even one's life is to come second to the decision to follow. Jesus said to "take up a cross" (Luke 14:26-27). His disciples would have been familiar with taking up a cross since the Romans of their day displayed this cruel form of punishment publicly. But the promise of the future for a disciple outweighed any cost, since the promise was for receiving much more in this life and of receiving eternal life in the world to come:

> Truly I say to you, there is no one who has left house or wife or brothers or parents or children, for the sake of the kingdom of God, who shall not receive many times as much at this time and in the age to come, eternal life. (Luke 18:29-30)

Just like the disciple who is not fit for the Kingdom if he looks back longingly for his former life, we have to realize that once we know the truth, life is meaningless without living it. We, in effect become like worthless salt. Salt is a preservative and a seasoning, but if it is ruined, it is worthless:

> Therefore, salt is good; but if even salt has become tasteless, with what will it be seasoned? It is useless either for the soil or for the manure pile; it is thrown out. He who has ears to hear, let him hear. (Luke 18:33-35)

Instead, we are to take this Kingdom message and be "lights for the world" and "salt for the earth." Our lights are to shine brightly so that we bring light to dark houses, to cities and nations. Our saltiness is to preserve the land on which we live and travel, safely securing it for those who come after us. Let us leave a godly inheritance and knowledge of this great King and His Kingdom.

CHAPTER SIX

KINGDOM LIVING KEYS

We are unworthy slaves; we have done only that which we ought to have done

The keys that follow all have one thing in common; they express the character of God. We cannot begin to summarize the greatness of God, or His attributes to any degree. He transcends all understanding. Saying "God is good" does not communicate the depth of this goodness, any more than saying "God is compassionate" describes the great tender mercies of His nature. Jesus demonstrated some of God's attributes as He preached the Kingdom, healed the sick (Matthew 4:23) and taught on Kingdom living. In portions throughout the gospel of Luke and in a compact section in Matthew 5-7, we see a picture of the Kingdom in operation. Jesus climbed a mountain and first taught what we call the "Beatitudes."

The first in Jesus' Kingdom Keys is: "Blessed are the poor in spirit, for theirs is the Kingdom of Heaven" (Matthew 5:3). This appears to be a look back at Isaiah. "But on this man will I look, even on him that is poor and of a contrite spirit, and trembles at My word" (Isa 66:2). One who trembles at God's Word is a person who will do it. This one is described as having a poor and contrite spirit. It takes humility to enter the Kingdom and live by its principles. Jesus said, "I assure you: Whoever does not welcome the kingdom of God like a little child will never enter it" (Luke 18:17 HCSB).

The second Kingdom Key is: "Blessed are those who mourn, for they be comforted." I believe the Lord is taking us to at least two places with this verse, which is also a parallelism to the prior verse. The poor in spirit are contrite and live rightly from the Word of God, those who mourn their sinful condition before God. Therefore, this verse is also about God's redemptive Kingdom and its salvation. The Lord takes us to Isaiah once more,

> To proclaim the year of the LORD'S good pleasure, and the day of vengeance of our God; **to comfort all that**

mourn, To appoint unto them that mourn in Zion, to give unto them a garland for ashes, the oil of joy for mourning, the mantle of praise for the spirit of heaviness; that they might be called terebinths of righteousness, the planting of the LORD, wherein He might glory. (Isa 61:2-3 JPS)

These are Messianic verses that Jesus' listeners would have immediately made a connection with by memory, and realized He was speaking of the Kingdom, and Himself, the Messiah, who would comfort the afflicted, the poor in spirit, and those who mourn by giving them a reason to rejoice, praise, and be planted in righteousness in the land.

The Third Kingdom Key: "Blessed are the gentle (meek, humble), for they shall inherit the earth" (Matthew 5:5 explanation added). This verse is also a parallelism of prior verses and loaded with hints back to the Psalms and other locations. For one, "But the humble shall inherit the land, and delight themselves in the abundance of peace." (Psa 37:11). Those who fear God, who tremble at His Word, have a deep sense of being accountable to Him, and are meek, humble and gentle. They mourn their spiritual condition apart from God, and they hunger for God's salvation. Jesus tells these—in my words, "The Kingdom is yours. You will inherit the land, and eternal life in the age to come."

Fourth: "Blessed are those who hunger and thirst for righteousness, for they shall be satisfied." (Matthew 5:6). In the Hebrew, which Jesus spoke, the words "salvation" and "righteousness" are often interchangeable. Notice Isaiah's parallelism, "He has clothed me in garments of salvation, He has wrapped me in a robe of righteousness" (Isaiah 62:10b). Isaiah is saying the same thing using two different words. Again Isaiah says, "I bring near My righteousness, it shall not be far off, and My salvation shall not tarry; and I will place salvation in Zion for Israel My glory" (Isa 46:13). When one truly understands the gift of righteousness from God, and operates in it, this one experiences salvation or wholeness.

Jesus, the Son of God, is the Great Prophet, and we should therefore attempt to interpret His words in the same manner as that of other prophets who spoke for God. He often spoke in parallelisms. In fact, much of what we call the Beatitudes contains parallelisms. We could also interpret this fourth key to say, "Blessed are those who hunger and thirst after salvation (who desire God's salvation more than food), they will be satisfied."

One of the covenant promises God made to Abraham was of land. The Jews were under Roman oppression and longed for the day when the Messiah would liberate them and they would have the right to their land once more. Jesus says, those who are poor in spirit, and mourn their condition—their sin, who are meek, and who are eager for God's salvation and righteousness, are blessed because God will give them their inheritance in the Kingdom.

Fifth: "Blessed are the merciful, for they shall receive mercy" (Matthew 5:7). The Lord quickens us to Isaiah again. This biblical text tells of mercy and kindness, charity and compassion. The text in Isaiah 58 shows mercy instead of sacrifice is what God desires. The concept of mercy toward one another is one of the main themes Jesus addresses in His teachings. The Hebrew concept of *Tzedakah* is righteous living exemplified in charity, love, giving, mercy, justice and much more. It is a Kingdom Key.

> *The Hebrew concept of tzedakah is righteous living exemplified in charity, love, giving, mercy and much more.*

Giving to the poor anonymously partially explains the highest form of *tzedakah*. *Tzedakah* as charity sums up all the commandments: "Love the Lord your God with all your heart, with all your soul, with all your strength, and with all your mind; and your neighbor as yourself" (Luke 10:27). God is very interested in how we treat one another, especially since God is in all of us. We are often doing unto God as we do unto others. Jesus said, "Just as you want others to do for you, do the same for them" (Luke 6:31). Righteousness must be viewed from God's perspective, which Jesus came to uphold. The following show just a couple of Old Testament verses the Lord quickened:

> Happy is one who cares for the poor; the LORD will save him in a day of adversity. The LORD will keep him and preserve him; he will be blessed in the land. You will not give him over to the desire of his enemies. (Psa 41:1-2)

> Is it not to share your bread with the hungry, to bring the poor and homeless into your house, to clothe the naked when you see him, and to not ignore your own flesh *and blood*? Then your light will appear like the dawn, and your recovery will come quickly. Your righteousness will go before you, and the LORD's glory will be your rear guard. At that time, when you call, the LORD will answer; when you cry out, He will say: Here I am. If you get rid of the yoke from those around you, the finger-pointing and malicious speaking, and if you offer yourself to the hungry, and satisfy the afflicted one, then your light will shine in the darkness, and your night will be like noonday. The LORD will always lead you, satisfy you in a parched land, and strengthen your bones. You will be like a watered garden and like a spring whose waters never run dry. Isa 58:7-11)

It is such as these who make up God's kingdom. Love, compassion and the flow of power are inseparable—"faith works by love" (Gal 5:6). Love precedes true power, which is itself a manifestation of the Kingdom. Jesus manifested His glory in His miracles—a demonstration of the Kingdom, and He fed the hungry.

Sixth: "Blessed are the pure in heart for they shall see God" (Matthew 5:8). The pure in heart are wholehearted. They fully love and serve Him and one another. They are free of sin—and are obedient from the heart (Rom 6:17). David sings:

> Who may ascend the mountain of the LORD? Who may stand in His holy place? The one who has clean hands and a pure heart, who has not set his mind on what is false, and who has not sworn deceitfully. (Psa 24:3–4)

The Essenes, who called themselves "sons of light", and who were monastic contemporaries of Jesus, eschewed worldliness, prized poverty, remained separate from Jewish life, and were a mystic sect of

Judaism. They considered "poor in spirit" a title of honor. The preacher of grace chants: "to proclaim to the meek the multitude of Thine mercies and to let them that are of contrite spirit to be nourished from the source of knowledge, and to them that mourn everlasting joy" (1QH18:14-15). We see a similarity with the teachings of Jesus. While it appears Jesus did not agree with all of the Essenes' theology, especially that of separation from society, He shows some similarities with their teachings.

Jesus specifically identified His mission as that of Isaiah 61:

> The Spirit of the Lord GOD is upon me, Because the LORD has anointed me to bring **good news** to the afflicted; He has sent me to bind up the brokenhearted, to proclaim liberty to captives, and freedom to prisoners; to proclaim the favorable year of the LORD, and the day of vengeance of our God; to comfort all who mourn, to grant those who mourn in Zion, giving them a garland instead of ashes, the oil of gladness instead of mourning, the mantle of praise instead of a spirit of fainting. So they will be called oaks of righteousness, the planting of the LORD, that He may be glorified. (Is. 61:1-3)

His call went to the poor in spirit, the meek, those who mourn and those who hunger after God's salvation. Many of these accepted Him as God's Messiah and salvation. I believe He preached from this passage in many synagogues, just as we see recorded for us in Luke:

> "The Spirit of the Lord is upon Me, Because He anointed Me to preach the gospel to the poor. He has sent Me to proclaim release to the captives, And recovery of sight to the blind, To set free those who are downtrodden, to proclaim the favorable year of the Lord." And He closed the book, and gave it back to the attendant, and sat down; and the eyes of all in the synagogue were fixed upon Him. And He began to say to them, "Today this Scripture has been fulfilled in your hearing." (Luke 4: 18-21)

The gospel, "good news," of the Kingdom is available for those who have a heart to receive it. It is fulfilled. The Lord's favor has dawned upon us.

THE KINGDOM LOVE KEY

The attributes of God, His character, are demonstrated in us, His children, when we act like Him. The Kingdom Keys that follow are about aspects of God's character that we are to imitate. "Walk in love" sums up this first Kingdom Key! Paul writes to the Ephesian church:

> Be ye therefore followers of God, as dear children; and walk in love, as Christ also hath loved us, and hath given himself for us an offering and a sacrifice to God for a sweetsmelling savour. (Eph. 5:1-2 KJV)

The Greek word for "followers" in this verse is *Mimetes* and means to mimic. So we are to be mimics of God, imitators (Strong 3402). Imitators impersonate the actions of others. Remember how children imitate the actions of their parents. They play in their shoes, dress up in their clothes, and say the same thing their parents say many times. That sums up how we should act. We are God's children and need to put on the new man who is created in the likeness and image of God: "Put on the new self, which in the likeness of God has been created in righteousness and holiness of the truth" (Ephes 4:24). If we love as He loves, we will imitate Him in every aspect of our lives. To "walk" refers to how we conduct ourselves. David sang, "Let the words of my mouth and the meditation of my heart be acceptable in Thy sight, O LORD, my rock and my Redeemer" (Psa 19:14). A bible scholar writes, "Let every act of life be dictated by love to God and man" (Clarke Eph 5:2).

The Lord's favor has dawned upon us.

In the world's system, we have a monetary currency that at one time was based on the gold standard. In God's Kingdom, the currency is faith. As I meditated on this truth, it seemed to me that I heard from the Lord, "The standard is love." The biblical text supports this:

"Faith works by love" (Galatians 5:6). I also heard, "Love operates the wheels of faith." Also, "A goal that aims at love won't miss," and, "Trust stems from love." Love is therefore the primary force expressing the Kingdom of Heaven. Lastly on this subject, I heard "Love is the basis for patience." We will be more patient with the shortcomings of others and ourselves when we realize patience is an act of love.

> *We must store up for ourselves "treasures in heaven." This is not just a reference to a future age but to an active spiritual dimension.*

We must store up for ourselves "treasures in heaven." This is not just a reference to a future age but to an active spiritual dimension. The Kingdom of Heaven is present when we are under God's reign. In His Kingdom, we sow and reap. We place stores in this dimension of the Spirit. Our acts of kindness, such as giving of charity, caring for orphans and widows, or prayer for the oppressed, places stores in the Kingdom of Heaven "where moth and rust do not destroy."

Acts of Kindness

In another passage in which Jesus teaches about "not serving two masters," a frequent theme we also see in Paul's writings, Jesus calls the "sons in light," (a reference to the Essenes, who regarded poverty as piety) less wise than the sons of the world. Jesus says to make friends for your self with money (Luke 16:8-12). Jesus' teachings show us that being poor in spirit, having true virtue, is hard to achieve when one is wealthy—being rich toward God is much preferred. Jesus tells us that trusting in riches is an obstacle to entering the Kingdom (Luke 18:25). We must trust in God, and maintain an attitude of stewardship. God and unrighteous mammon are two masters. We must choose whom we serve. This is a hard task for those of us who live in such an affluent society, and have security in our jobs and bank accounts. Jesus is saying that we have to trust God, enough so that our giving (making friends with money), takes a higher value in our lives than possessions. He says, "life does not consist in an abundance of one's possessions" (Luke 12:15). In the story of the rich man and Lazarus, Jesus again shows how the roles are reversed in the age to come; the rich man is in eternal torment, and the beggar, Lazarus, in eternal security (Luke 16:19).

In studying the sayings of Jesus, He points toward a time when the roles of the outcasts, the mournful, and oppressed are reversed with those of the rich (Luke 6:24-26). The first becomes last and the last first. James, the Lord's brother carries this theme in his epistle:

> Let the lowly brother glory in his exaltation, but the rich in his humiliation, because as a flower of the field he will pass away. For no sooner has the sun risen with a burning heat than it withers the grass; its flower falls, and its beautiful appearance perishes. So the rich man also will fade away in his pursuits. (James 1:9-11)

It is difficult not to see that the Lord saw wealth and possessions as an obstacle to entering the Kingdom. As with many who hide themselves from the world to find intimacy with God, Jesus often pulled away to spend time with God. Those who choose to live a reclusive lifestyle focused on prayer, mostly live a spartan existence. It may not be that Jesus saw poverty as the ideal, but rather wealth and possessions as distractions. He described "the deceitfulness of riches" as that which chokes the Word, and thereby, its fruitfulness.

Jesus desired that His followers store up treasures in Heaven—the spiritual realm. To the rich young ruler, He said, "You still lack one thing. Sell all that you have and distribute to the poor, and you will have treasure in heaven; and come, follow Me" (Luke 18:22). I see in this passage that Jesus looked at this man (one gospel says "loved him") and spoke to him directly:

> How hard it is for those who have riches to enter the kingdom of God! For it is easier for a camel to go through the eye of a needle than for a rich man to enter the kingdom of God. (Luke 18:24-25)

Can you imagine Jesus looking into your eyes and saying, "how hard it is for a rich man to enter the Kingdom of Heaven?" It must be very difficult to always put the Kingdom of Heaven first when one is wealthy! Paul instructed his young disciple Timothy on the same subject:

> Instruct those who are rich in this present world not to be conceited or to fix their hope on the uncertainty of riches, but on God, who richly supplies us with all things to enjoy. Instruct them to do good, to be rich in good works, to be generous and ready to share, storing up for themselves the treasure of a good foundation for the future, so that they may take hold of that which is life indeed. (1Tim. 6:17)

We must see that when we store up treasures in the spiritual realm, it creates abundance in this life and the next. These things are available, just out of sight! In such a land of abundance, we often fail to see how driven we are to obtain and hoard. I heard in the spirit realm:

> They spend money they do not have,
> To buy what they cannot afford,
> To fulfill a desire,
> They cannot satisfy.

Does this not sum up America's penchant for credit cards and possessions? The average person gives little and charges much! Yes, and all this drive for wealth will not satisfy.

The early followers of Jesus took His teachings literally. Luke's account in the book of Acts shows us that they "sold their possessions and goods, and divided them among all, as anyone had need" (Acts 2:45). The Apostle Paul was constantly taking up collections for the poor in Jerusalem. Giving to the poor, sharing abundance so that all had their needs met, and sacrificial living, characterized the early church. The Jews understood God's blessings as a stewardship, and that the poor had a "right" to a share in the blessings of those whom God blessed. In the same sense, the poor knew according to God's commands, they had the right to receive support for their needs.

> When you reap the harvest of your land, moreover, you shall not reap to the very corners of your field, nor gather the gleaning of your harvest; you are to leave them for the needy and the alien. I am the LORD your God. (Lev. 23:22)

To Hear is to Do

Jesus spoke strongly about hearing His teachings and not doing them. It amounts to not listening at all if we do not do as He says. He speaks these strong words after giving His discourse that we call the "Beatitudes," along with a lengthy teaching on loving without bounds. Listen to His warning:

> And He also spoke a parable to them: "A blind man cannot guide a blind man, can he? Will they not both fall into a pit? A pupil is not above his teacher; but everyone, after he has been fully trained, will be like his teacher. And why do you look at the speck that is in your brother's eye, but do not notice the log that is in your own eye? Or how can you say to your brother, 'Brother, let me take out the speck that is in your eye,' when you yourself do not see the log that is in your own eye? You hypocrite, first take the log out of your own eye, and then you will see clearly to take out the speck that is in your brother's eye. For there is no good tree which produces bad fruit; nor, on the other hand, a bad tree which produces good fruit. For each tree is known by its own fruit. For men do not gather figs from thorns, nor do they pick grapes from a briar bush. The good man out of the good treasure of his heart brings forth what is good; and the evil man out of the evil treasure brings forth what is evil; for his mouth speaks from that which fills his heart. And why do you call Me, 'Lord, Lord,' and do not do what I say? Everyone who comes to Me, and hears My words, and acts upon them, I will show you whom he is like: he is like a man building a house, who dug

deep and laid a foundation upon the rock; and when a flood rose, the torrent burst against that house and could not shake it, because it had been well built. But the one who has heard, and has not acted accordingly, is like a man who built a house upon the ground without any foundation; and the torrent burst against it and immediately it collapsed, and the ruin of that house was great. (Luke 6:39-49)

Love is the foremost Kingdom Key

God is Love. Love does no wrong to its neighbor—and loving without bounds is the way God loves: "Therefore, you must love without bounds, as your Heavenly Father loves" (Matt 5:48 NJB). Once more the Message Bible captures this picture:

In a word, what I'm saying is, *Grow up*. You're kingdom subjects. Now live like it. Live out your God-created identity. Live generously and graciously toward others, the way God lives toward you. (Matt 5:48 MSG)

Being "generous to a fault" is a cliché we have heard. God wants our generosity, our love, or charity, to be without bounds. We must hold nothing too tightly, but recognize we are stewards: the King has left us in charge while He is away. Jesus tells a story of a certain man who left his servants in charge and comes back unexpectedly: "He said therefore, A certain

> *Love is the foremost Kingdom Key.*

nobleman went to a distant country to receive a kingdom for himself, and then return'" (Luke 19:12). While the king is away, he gives his servants money to invest, to do business. One translation says that man tells his servants to "occupy" until I come. Some acted wisely and received more upon the king's return: one acted unwisely, and lost everything. As stewards of God's blessings, Kingdom living demands we are to act wisely.

Peter explains when we have done all the things we should do, we will have gained a great advantage in the eternal kingdom:

Therefore, brethren, be all the more diligent to make certain about His calling and choosing you; for as long as you practice these things, you will never stumble; for in this way the entrance into the eternal kingdom of our Lord and Savior Jesus Christ will be abundantly supplied to you. (1 Peter 1:10-11)

CHAPTER SEVEN

KEYS THAT CONTINUE TO UNLOCK BIG DOORS

Without love, I am nothing

The righteousness of *tzedakah*, unbounded love and charity, is a key that must become a lifestyle with us. When we practice *tzedakah,* the unseen realities of the Kingdom of Heaven are at work in and for us. We are not sinning because "Love does no wrong to a neighbor; love therefore is the fulfillment of the law" (Rom. 13:10). The righteousness that is fulfilled in love is also called the "royal law." "If, however, you are fulfilling the royal law,

> *The righteousness of tzedakah, unbounded love and charity, must become a lifestyle for us.*

according to the Scripture, 'You shall love your neighbor as yourself,' you are doing well'" (James 2:8). By the Holy Spirit given to us, we fulfill all the royal law requires of us. Believers seem to try to hold God in awe and think they are right with Him, when it is impossible to be in harmony with God when one is not in harmony with God's family. Jesus said in a number of teachings that we had to be right with our neighbors before we could be set-right with God. In the following, He relates it to worship:

> Therefore if you bring your gift to the altar, and there remember that your brother has something against you, leave your gift there before the altar, and go your way. First be reconciled to your brother, and then come and offer your gift. (Matt. 5:23-24)

Hebrews tells us: "Therefore, since we receive a kingdom which cannot be shaken, let us show gratitude, by which we may offer to God an acceptable service with reverence and awe" (Heb 12:28). With so many blessings, let us be grateful. Let us share His love "shed abroad in our hearts by the Holy Spirit" (Romans 5:5).

Doors in the Kingdom Still Swing on Hinges of God's Love

God desired to reach out to us in love, and draw us near, but we were too full of ourselves, sin-and-flesh-ruled-people. God is Holy—we would be consumed. God acted in the person of Jesus to bring us near, to reconcile us to Himself through Christ (Rom 5:1). Because of who He is and what He did, through the faithfulness of Jesus Christ, God imputed righteousness to us. God's righteous nature, His saving justice and fair judgment, is manifest in Christ. He became to us the wisdom of God, righteousness, sanctification and redemption (1Cor 1:30).

I am convinced, when we understand and experience the love of God, the love He has for us that caused Him to give His Son for us, we will begin to receive it and experience wholeness. Knowing we are made righteous through the faith of Jesus means that we are saved, healed, whole, delivered, freed, removed from danger, and prospered. You will recall Jesus' words about the lost—those who are lost, broken, and sick. We must pick up His mission. We are fully loved and equally partnered with Christ—to rule through righteousness. Sin used to reign, but now righteousness reigns through Christ (Rom 5:21).

In Jesus' day, they longed for freedom from Roman rule, for God's Kingdom to come. This meant to them an earthly Kingdom free of any rule apart from God's:

> The greater, then, the oppression of the Worldly Kingdom (Rome), the more eager the Jewish people, particularly the pious ones, were for "the Kingdom of Heaven," as they called it, to come speedily. This is the ever-reiterated object of the prayers in the liturgy (Masseket Soferim, xiv. 12; *et al.*). It was even laid down that no benediction would be effective without reference to the Kingdom (Ber. 12a). It is the approach of this Kingdom of Heaven, in opposition to the Kingdom of Rome . . . and when he (Jesus) said, "the kingdom of God cometh not by observation [that is, calculation] . . . for, behold, the kingdom of God is

among [not within] you" (Luke xvii. 21, Syriac version), he meant, "It does not come through rebellion or by force" (Jewish Encyclopedia)

As persecution came, and in the same manner comes to us in this age, some saw the Kingdom of Heaven as an escape. Kingdom living is about abundant life! Christianity needs to stop being about death—waiting for Heaven, the age to come. This is extremely selfish, and therefore lacking in righteousness. Most who say they are ready to go home, and hang their head because of sorrow or tribulation, are not really longing to see the Lord, but wanting to escape this gift of life. We need to experience life in the here and now—resurrection life, and the abundant life Jesus came to give us. It does not mean we are free of trials and tests, but Jesus said to overcome because He has overcome, "You must find your peace in Me. In this world, you will experience tribulation. Be courageous; I have overcome the world" (John 16:33 My translation).

Living under God's reign—the kingdom—means we have all of what God intends, free of strife, walking in love and fellowship. To be a disciple means we become like our teacher. We become deliverers. Jesus expected His disciples to be like Him and to do His works. That is why He upbraided Peter when his faith failed; he began to sink after joining Jesus as He walked on water (Mat 14:31). We must be like Him who offers us the Kingdom: "It is enough for a disciple to become like his teacher and a slave like his master" (Mat 10:25a).

To be like our Master, we must first receive His love—learn to know God. Flusser says that which Jesus recognized and desired is fulfilled in the message of the Kingdom:

> There God's unconditional love for all becomes visible, and the barriers between sinner and righteous are shattered. Human dignity becomes null and void, the last become first, and the first become last. The poor, the hungry, the meek, the mourners, and the persecuted inherit the Kingdom of Heaven (God). In Jesus' message of the Kingdom, the strictly social factor does not, however, seem to be the decisive thing. His

revolution has to do chiefly with the transvaluation of all the usual moral values, and hence his promises are especially for sinners. "Truly, I say to you, the tax collectors and the harlots go into the kingdom of God before you" (Matt 21:31-32). The message of the Kingdom resonated among the social outcasts and the despised, just as John the Baptist's. (Flusser 111-112)

Jesus' message of love embraces even those who were viewed as enemies. He wanted not to overthrow Rome and be crowned King, but to see God's kingdom become inclusive. The ethics of the Kingdom principle of love is more powerful than that of the kingdom of darkness and its selfishness and oppression. Flusser explains that Jesus' message of love and non-violence instead of hatred toward enemies would triumph and ultimately avoid provoking the Roman Empire to attack:

Because Satan and his powers will be overthrown, and the present world-order shattered (of which Rome was a world-order at that time), it is to be regarded almost with indifference, and not to be strengthened by opposition. For when the Kingdom of God is fully realized, all this will vanish. (Flusser 112)

Jesus also warned His people that they missed the hour of their visitation (see Luke 19). His message was to the Jews—the lost sheep of the house of Israel, who were to take the light to the world. We have been grafted into this holy root of Israel, and because we have failed to understand this, we fail to grasp the Kingdom message. The Scriptures show us, God is inclusive, and we are invited to experience His love and the reconciliation Christ provided.

Jesus seems to argue against rebellion to Rome, rather "love your enemies." Rather than delivering from Rome's dominion, Jesus wants to deliver from Satan's oppression. I would summarize in these words, "Do not resist Rome, but resist evil." Peter says Jesus "went about doing good and healing all who were oppressed of the devil for God was with Him" (Acts 10:38). Satan can only oppress with limited access. Jesus brought an end to Satan's efforts to enslave through sin and fear of death. With Jesus' sin offering on our behalf, and His death and resurrection, God sent the Holy Spirit in His name. The empowerment of the Holy Spirit is the power to resist and overcome evil.

Opposition to evil, and provoking the wrath of one's enemies is to be avoided. Unfortunately, while many Jews heeded the teachings of Jesus, believed in Him and followed Him, and His disciples after Him (e.g., 3,000 on Pentecost), the Jewish leaders and resistance forces did not all heed this message of the Kingdom. They failed to recognize their hour of visitation. Rome destroyed the Temple and Jerusalem forty years after Jesus' pronouncement: "They will crush you and your children within you to the ground, and they will not leave one stone on another in you, because you did not recognize the time of your visitation" (Luke 19:44).

Love without bounds is the opposite of Self-love that makes one selfish and self-centered. Self-centeredness is indicative of living outside the kingdom. When we understand love, God's love, and how we are made righteous by the faithfulness of Jesus, we can experience wholeness—it will overtake us. We begin to live for God and for others—just like our Master Jesus. This amounts to understanding our purpose in life—loving God and others. When we get over ourselves, and seek the Kingdom, we will have made great progress in this life.

> *Love without bounds is the opposite of Self-love that makes one selfish and self-centered..*

Jesus restored our kingly authority, the sphere of influence we lost in Eden. He came to restore what we failed to be able to do through keeping the law—the law had no power to cause us to live righteously—it showed us the mark of righteous living. In the Kingdom, we face the same issues as Adam and Eve in their environment, but with the Holy Spirit's power. By the Spirit, we now have power to overcome the flesh, to become whole. God's rule, His dominion, over our bodies, minds, hearts, marriages, and all relationships in the Kingdom means the authority of God will be exercised through us, His "viceroys" and "Kings." We have God's Spirit to guide us as we rule and reign through Christ.

> *Self-centeredness is indicative of living outside the kingdom.*

The kingdom is not in a certain place in this age, but it is the presence of God's rule in our lives manifested in grace, His people, and His power working on our behalf. Through God's love in Christ, His gift of grace, we can "taste and see the Lord is good." We can experience Him in the here and now, not just in the world to come. With His empowerment, we can live lives worthy of the King. When we live outside the kingdom—we do not come into contact with God's power. We live darkened lives because we lack kingdom living.

As reiterated, the Kingdom of Heaven, the *Malkut Shamayim*, is Jesus' main theme, and He demonstrates the kingdom after teaching on it by freeing people from sickness and unclean spirits. His second theme, which is a part of living in the kingdom, is a righteous way of living. It is the spiritual principles of the law—love God and your neighbor as yourself. True *tzedakah* is righteousness demonstrated in charity. When we receive Christ based on His faithfulness to God through His life, death and resurrection, we have the power to live in the Kingdom.

> *When we live outside the kingdom—we do not come into contact with God's power.*

We are able to live on the spiritual plane, instead of the so much of the physical. We live in the Spiritual dimension and the natural, and we bring to pass those things we desire in the natural, by a spiritual means.

While Jesus' brethren knew the Holy Scriptures and sought to know God and live righteously, Jesus came to show that they had to exceed the righteousness of the scribes and Pharisees. He interpreted the scriptures to show God's standard of righteousness had to be of the heart, not just an action of doing the commands, but unconditional love. He said, love not only your brother, but also your enemies. He put the standards that the Scriptures sought to bring man up to, even higher. When we live in love, then "the Kingdom of God is not eating and drinking, but righteousness, shalom, and joy in the Holy Spirit" (Rom 14:17 HNV).

THE KINGDOM FAITH KEY

Everything in me reverberates with the truth that the Kingdom of Heaven is the spiritual realm, or we can say, the spiritual dimension. Some have seen into this dimension and beheld Jesus, God (not fully, or we could not handle it), angels, and "heard inexpressible words, which a man is not permitted to speak." Paul was transported to this dimension and called it Paradise, the third Heaven. "And I know how such a man — whether in the body or apart from the body I do not know, God knows—was caught up into Paradise, and heard inexpressible words, which a man is not permitted to speak" (2 Cor 12:3-4). Some have beheld Heaven—the Paradise Paul writes about. Some have beheld angels and received revelations. Others have had open visions, dreams and visions of things unseen. When we pray, declare or decree by the Spirit of God in us, we are in touch with this dimension. As noted earlier, prayer is the prime conduit for this establishment in our lives of the unseen realities of God's Kingdom. Yes, we can also ascend into the spiritual realm when God calls us higher. In union with God's Spirit, we can tap into this parallel spiritual dimension and create our own reality; through faith, we encounter and activate God's supernatural abilities to declare "those things that be not as though they were."

The spiritual is the pattern for the natural. When we have "close encounters" with this realm, we know His Presence in a more physical way—the boundaries in the spiritual dimension and the physical blur. I sometimes think we forget where we end and God's Spirit begins—His Presence so envelops us. The cloud of His Presence is visible to the eye as He chooses to manifest His Presence more in the seen realm. Believe me, when you have seen into the spiritual realm, and beheld the holes the nails left in the hands of the Resurrected Lord and light shining through them, your life is forever different. When the room fills with the fog or cloud of His Presence, you forget this present world. When you have been lifted up in a chariot of some kind, and angels surround you as you ascend, you stop doubting God is at work in a supernatural way, and the things of God become even more precious. You "sell out."

Recently, Dr. Bracken Christian[3], my son and Pastor, related hearing the Spirit say, "I have called you into a deeper dimension." I believe this is the dimension of the Spirit. God is disclosing a plan to

---

[3] Dr. Bracken Christian is "faith teacher" extraordinaire, and I owe him much for his consistent approach to the biblical text and to obeying a command to teach faith and vision. Dr. Christian's ministry information is found at www.fhclubbock.org.

entrust more of His Spirit to him in a dimension of understanding in a spectacular way.

But even if we never experience the supernatural in greater measure, we can operate in faith that it exists and live accordingly by faith. The Lord expects it. After a teaching on prayer, Jesus says, "When the Son of Man comes will He find faith?"

The Kingdom of Heaven then, and the Heaven Jesus spoke about, is the spiritual realm, what I have termed "the dimension of unseen realities." As I began work on this section about the Faith Key, the Holy Spirit led me to this translation of a verse in the New Jerusalem Bible that caps my understanding of the unseen realities of the Kingdom of Heaven—He amazes me! "Only faith can guarantee the blessings that we hope for, or prove the existence of realities that are unseen" (Heb. 11:1 NJB). Faith is that aspect of God revealed when God calls those things that be not as though they were: "God, who gives life to the dead and calls into being that which does not exist" (Romans 4:17). Listen to this truth by biblical writers:

> By faith we understand that the worlds were prepared by the word of God, so that what is seen was not made out of things which are visible (seen) (Hebrews 11:3) By faith Noah, being warned by God about things not yet seen, in reverence prepared an ark for the salvation of his household, by which he condemned the world, and became an heir of the righteousness which is according to faith (Hebrews 11:7). By faith he (Moses) left Egypt, not fearing the wrath of the king; for he endured, as **seeing Him who is unseen**. (Hebrews 11:27) while we look not at the things which are seen, but at **the things which are not seen**; for the things which are seen are temporal, but the things which are **not seen are eternal** (2 Cor 4:18) (Emphasis added).

A fiat is a formal or official authorization of something, an authoritative and often arbitrary command (Encarta). God works by fiat, speaking and creating something from nothing—He declared us righteous in Christ. Past perfect tense: "Therefore having been justified by faith, we have peace with God through our Lord Jesus

Christ" (Romans 5:1). God speaks oracles, and they cannot be changed. Since we are created in His image and likeness, as a speaking spirit, we must declare and decree in fiat as well. We must be like Him.

Walk by Faith and Not by Sight

The faith life demands of us that we do not live by the things we see, for they are temporal. We live by faith. "For he who comes to God must believe that He is, and that He is a rewarder of those who seek Him" (Hebrews 11:6). Were we to base our lives on only what our eyes see, we could not be able to accomplish what God desires of us. We serve God whom we cannot see to accomplish what we cannot see, but receive by faith. I remind you that in God's Kingdom, the currency is faith and the standard for that currency is love. And, Love operates the wheels of faith. If we are to "walk by faith and not by sight," then we are not walking (living) by our five senses, but by the Word of God and the Spirit of God in us. (2 Cor 5:7). Our circumstances may appear bleak, but our faith insists that we overcome. Our faith may "make" us continue to believe for and expect to obtain what looks impossible. Jesus said to Martha, "Did I not say to you that if you would believe you will see the glory of God" (John 11:40).

Many times Jesus told those who sought Him for healing or deliverance, "Your faith has saved you," or, "Your faith has made you whole." In fact, more often than not, Jesus said the person's faith was the reason they received healing and wholeness. As I mentioned earlier, many who came to Him, were not looking for salvation as we think of it, an entrance into the world to come or "Heaven." They believed Jesus could heal them, make them whole. When they cried out in faith, He healed them. Two accounts in the biblical text show us that Jesus commended great faith. To the Roman Centurion who recognized authority and asked Jesus to just speak the word so his servant would be healed, and a Canaanite woman who persisted until Jesus healed her daughter of a demon, Jesus gave His highest compliment on faith. Yet His own disciples, He often rebuked for their lack of faith. From these accounts (Matthew 8), we can see that great faith believes completely in God's ability and willingness to heal, even at a distance by just speaking the word, and does not give up.

Just as the Lord expects His followers to be persistent in prayer, He expects His followers to be persistent in faith. Prayer is an act of faith in itself, and persistent prayer demonstrates greater faith. Bible expositors have labeled this kind of faith in prayer, importunity. It is persistent stick-to-it-ness, tenacious prayer. This faith believes that God is who He said He is and God will do what He said He would do.

Jesus operated in Kingdom faith and power. After being anointed by the Holy Spirit, He performed many miracles and healings, and He expected His disciples to be like Him. He sent them out to do what they had seen Him do; He gave them authority. He said that it takes very small faith to move a mountain! (Mark 11:23-24). If we truly understood the authority and power delegated to us, then we would do "greater works" than Jesus did, just as He said we would do. The authority to "tread on serpents and scorpions and over all the power of the enemy" (Luke 10:19) grants us power over evil spirits that are unseen. In this dimension and present age, we see only the effect of such spirits, but if we have the gift of discernment, we can see into this realm. As well as angels who are on our side, we would see those against us. The Prophet Elisha prayed that his servant would see the unseen reality of a mighty number of angels who were on their side against an enemy's army. Elisha prayed, "'LORD, I pray, open his eyes that he may see.' Then the LORD opened the eyes of the young man, and he saw. And behold, the mountain was full of horses and chariots of fire all around Elisha" (2 Kings 6:17).

> *Great faith believes completely in God's ability and willingness to heal, even at a distance by just speaking the word, and does not give up.*

Faithfulness

"Faithfulness" is a concept that is meant in many places in the biblical text where translators have used the word "faith." What is faithfulness? God's character is described in part by the term faithfulness. This kingdom key is likewise an attribute ascribed to

God: "Great is Your faithfulness" (Lam 3:23). Jesus demonstrated faithfulness throughout His life and ministry. He is the "faithful and true witness." Faithfulness is described as that attribute of being consistently trustworthy, loyal, and true, especially to a promise.

The Lord gave a number of examples of the "faithful servant." "Blessed are those servants whom the master, when he comes, will find watching. Assuredly, I say to you that he will gird himself and have them sit down to eat, and will come and serve them" (Luke 12:37). The faithful servant is one who is watchful and "keeps his lamp full," and does not compromise his faith. We watch well in prayer.

Aesop wrote fables some 600 years before Christ. One of them that is preserved is about an oak and a reed. The learned Rabbi that He was, Jesus would have been familiar with such stories. It speaks of faithfulness and refusal to compromise. Jesus uses one to communicate a point about John the Baptist, his uncompromising stance. It is a lesson for us as well. The original fable is translated as:

> A very large Oak was uprooted by the wind and thrown across a stream. It fell among some Reeds, which it thus addressed: "I wonder how you, who are so light and weak, are not entirely crushed by these strong winds." They replied, "You fight and contend with the wind, and consequently you are destroyed; while we on the contrary bend before the least breath of air, and therefore remain unbroken, and escape."

It is better to be uprooted than to bend to every wind or doctrine. In describing John, Jesus said, "What did you go out into the desert to gaze on? A reed shaken and swayed by the wind?" (Luke 7:24). John would break before he compromised the word of the Lord, and Herod ordered him beheaded for it. Shadrach, Meshach, and Abed-nego remained faithful and would not compromise. They refused to bow to a golden image, confident God would rescue them from a fiery furnace—He did! Daniel remained faithful and refused to cease his prayers. God rescued him from the lions' den. Joseph remained faithful and refused to yield to the wife of Potiphar and her seduction. When falsely accused and thrown into prison, God was with him and he prospered. Jesus, our ultimate example, remained faithful after a forty day fast. He remained steadfast when Satan tempted him to deny his faith and obedience to God's word—He overcame by the Word. The book of Hebrews reminds us that Jesus was tempted in the same way as we are except He remained faithful: "For we do not have a High Priest who cannot sympathize with our weaknesses, but was in all points tempted as we are, yet without sin" (Heb. 4:15).

THE KINGDOM JOY KEY

Faith has an attitude of joy. Paul wrote a joyous letter to the Philippians and commended them for their joy in the faith: "I shall remain and continue with you all for your progress and joy in the faith" (Phil 1:25). One translation says "joy in believing." Believing produces joy. When you know you have been redeemed from sin's slave market and transferred into the Kingdom of God's Son, it should produce joy. In fact, believers should be the most joyful people in the world. We have salvation and should draw joyously from these springs (Isa 12:3).

I believe God does not enjoy us much in our times of self-pity and sorrow. He wants us to have joy! I further believe the Lord is not the mad and sad God many portray, but longs to rejoice over us: "The LORD your God is in your midst, A victorious warrior. **He will exult over you with joy, He will be quiet in His love, He will rejoice over you with shouts of joy**" (Zeph 3:17). In Deuteronomy He tells the Israelites how He delights in prospering them:

> Then the LORD your God will prosper you abundantly in all the work of your hand, in the offspring of your body and in the offspring of your cattle and in the produce of your ground, for the LORD will again **rejoice over you for good**, just as He rejoiced over your fathers. (Deut. 30:9)

We often use Paul's prison letter to the Philippians, which is full of the words "joy" and "rejoice," as an example of how we should respond in difficulties. In a similar way, in the midst of tribulation,

James and Peter both encourage us to rejoice, and rejoice greatly! (James 1:2, 1 Peter 1:6). Faith rejoices! Circumstances are a lot more bearable when we choose to rejoice. It is our strength (Neh 8:10). Listen to Peter:

> And though you have not seen Him, you love Him, and though you do not see Him now, but believe in Him, you greatly rejoice with joy inexpressible and full of glory. (1Pet 1:8)

In the Lord, we have such joy. The Holy Spirit in us is full of joy and will express His joy through us if we would but let Him. I remind you, "The Kingdom of God is righteousness, joy and peace in the Holy Spirit."

If you find you have lost your joy, you have more than likely lost your faith and peace. They form a threefold cord. David asked God to restore the joy that he had lost: "Restore to me the joy of Thy salvation, and sustain me with a willing spirit" (Psa 51:12). If you look up a few verses on joy, it will be contagious. You will smile and rejoice. "Put on the garment of praise" and you will begin to rejoice; at first by your will, but then by a willing spirit.

THE KINGDOM PEACE KEY

Supernatual peace guards our hearts and minds when we stay in the Spirit. Whether by prayer where we go before God and leave our concerns with Him, or by speakng the word over ourselves and obtaining peace, it is available. The biblical text often uses words repetitiously to communicate the extent of the word's meaning. For example, God is holy, holy, holy. His holiness is transcendent. In Isaiah, we read a verse containing peace, peace. This indicates loads of peace. It is like being in the rain, rain (experiencing lots of it). The Lord says of peace in Isaiah: "The steadfast of mind Thou wilt keep in perfect peace, because he trusts in Thee" (Isa 26:3). Literally this verse is saying, "God will keep us in peace peace when we keep our minds on Him and trust Him." Trust is another word for faith, and similiar to joy, salvation produces extreme peace and security in us. "The mind stayed on the Spirit is life and peace" (Romans 8:6).

Peace is the word *"shalom"* in Hebrew. Shalom amounts to prosperity—a sense of well-being, completeness, soundness, health, and safety (Strong 7965). It is summed up in nothing missing, nothing broken. God desired us to have the peace lost in Eden, peace with Him, within ourselves, with others, and with our environment. Isaiah tells us that peace and righteousness are related: "The work of righteousness will be shalom; and the effect of righteousness, quietness and confidence forever" (Isaiah 32:17 HNV). Righteousness leads to sustained peace—peace of mind. That is what Jesus gave us through His atonement. "Therefore, being justified by faith, we have peace with God through our Lord Jesus Christ" (Romans 5:1). Justification means that you have been made right with God. You can stand before Him fully righteous in Christ without fear of judgment. This is peace, and it is rest to a weary soul.

THE KINGDOM HOPE KEY

Hope is so misunderstood. Often we can ask a person a question that requires faith, they will say, "I hope so." This kind of hope is based on feelings and sight, not faith. Bible hope is a different kind of hope. Bible hope is based on the promises of God. We often read in the New Testament of our "Blessed Hope." This looks to a fulfillment of a promise of the appearing of our Lord and the culmination of our hope and trust in Him. This Bible kind of hope may be compared to the promises that are in God, which faith takes hold of and brings into manifestation. It has been said, and I paraphrase, "Hope is like a rope that is tied to the Mercy Seat, and faith pulls on that rope until the promise is secured." I like this analogy, because often we do not see God's promises as immutable, but they are.

Abraham is a great example of this kind of hope: "Who in hope believed against hope, to the end that he might become a father of many nations, according to that which had been spoken, "So will your seed be" (Rom 4:18 HNV). Because of His faith—agreeing with what God said, and not wavering, "God reckoned Abraham righteous." Abraham looked to the hope of God's promise in faith. Abraham believed, not by looking at what was impossible in his own flesh, but what was possible in God. We only doubt when we look at ourselves and not at God's promises and greatness.

THE KINGDOM HUMILITY KEY

The measure for measure concept applies to all areas of our lives, with God and with man. The universal laws of sowing and reaping (giving and receiving or cause and affect) are immutable. For example, God gave His Son and effected reconciliation—reaping His family. Jesus often spoke of opposites that rendered a result. The prideful will be humbled, and the humble will be exalted.

The Master removed His outer garment, put on a towel, and served His disciples by washing their feet, the act of a lowly house servant. This acted parable demonstrated the humility of the Lord, who came to Earth having first removed His garments of glory and empting Himself (Phil 2:8). A third at the cross, the Romans stripped Him of His garments. He hung naked and distanced from those who loved Him, even though He could have called legions of angels to help. Contrast this act of humility with His disciples who twice argued about who was the greatest, the latter as He ate His last meal with them (Luke 9:46, 22:24). Jesus said to them:

> Whoever is greatest among you must become like the youngest, and whoever leads, like the one serving; For whoever is least among you—this one is great. Whoever exalts himself will be humbled, and whoever humbles himself will be exalted. (Luke 22:26, 9:48; Matt 23:12)

Jesus gave other examples of humility as opposed to pride. He contrasted the Pharisee and the tax collector at prayer, and how the Pharisee prayed with himself as he recounted his righteous acts! Yet the tax collector went home justified, because he humbled himself before God (Luke 18:10-14).

Humility is the opposite of arrogance, which exalts itself, and is self-seeking. Humility has an aspect of respect, and meekness toward others—it is acting in accordance with truth. James and John tried to position themselves at Jesus' right and left hand, positions of honor in the kingdom. They stooped to the level of having their mother go to Jesus for the request (Matt 20:20-28). This is self-seeking at its worst—as the Master speaks of His suffering and death on their behalf, this pair of disciples are seeking positions of power, and arguing who is the greatest and therefore most deserving of a position!

When we seek our own way, we lift ourselves up above God who has told us His ways. Also, we must lift ourselves up to look down on others. This is a dangerous position. We are safest when we remain in the circle of love. The humility key opens the doors to greatness. We unlock and walk through doors of faith by using this key.

THE KINGDOM WISDOM KEY

Wisdom is the source of all knowledge and understanding. "It is the principal thing, therefore get wisdom . . ." (Prov 4:7). This wisdom is from God, Who is the source of all—He is Father, which can mean Source. Wisdom is light, as is knowledge and truth. Therefore, true knowledge of God has to begin from wisdom. You can recognize wisdom by its character. It is free of all darkness. Adam Clarke writes:

> The (God) source of wisdom, knowledge, holiness, and happiness; and in him is no darkness at all—no ignorance, no imperfection, no sinfulness, no misery. And from him wisdom, knowledge, holiness, and happiness are received by every believing soul. (Clarke "1 John 1:5")

Paul describes it:

> But the wisdom from above is first pure, then peaceable, gentle, reasonable, full of mercy and good fruits, unwavering, without hypocrisy. (James 3:17)

This wisdom is supernatural. It has the ability within it to reproduce its character. It is at best described as divine inspiration or divine ability. Solomon excelled in this gift from God. It is also available to those of us who are priests and kings by God's grace.

If wisdom is life, then it produces light, illumination, and shows us the way to live, and is in essence truth. Thus if we are to grasp truth, we must have wisdom. It follows that God is the God of truth (Isa 65:16, Ps 31:5); Jesus said, I am the way, the truth, and the life (John 14:6); His Word is truth (John 17:17); He has given us the Spirit of Truth (John 15:26); God is light and His Son, the Light of the world while He as in the world (1 John 1:5, John 8:12). **To gain wisdom, we must therefore ask God for it, and begin with truth, which is the Word of God, gain knowledge and understanding of it, and it will produce life and light when we understand and apply it (walk in it).** "The unfolding of Thy words gives light; it gives understanding to the simple" (Psa 119:130). We are God's wicks, and He lights our lamps using the oil of His Holy Spirit and His Word of truth. It produces in us the light of His Presence, the very Shekinah. When we walk in the wisdom of this light, of this knowledge and understanding, "the blood of Jesus His Son cleanses us from all sin" (1 John 1:7). We must walk in the light! Remember, to hear is to do. Applying knowledge of truth amounts to doing the Word. It is an act of faith. Remember that wisdom is something greater; it is the fountain bubbling up from God.

Throughout the Proverbs, wisdom cries out to us, giving examples of the benefits of wisdom, and of applying it. Often it is associated with finding life. James says we should ask for wisdom: "But if any of you lacks wisdom, let him ask of God, who gives to all men generously and without reproach, and it will be given to him" (James 1:5).

When we gain Christ, we can see that as the manifested Word of God, the truth, life, and light, He becomes God's wisdom to us—God's truth, life, and light. Paul explains: "But of Him you are in Christ Jesus, who became for us wisdom from God—and righteousness and sanctification and redemption" (1Cor. 1:30). We can walk in this wisdom and continually live in light, receiving His ability and power.

CHAPTER EIGHT

THE NARROW ENTRANCE INTO THE KINGDOM

*He brought me into a broad place, but first
I had to squeeze through the narrow entrance*

Jesus' teachings contain an element of how difficult it is to enter the Kingdom of Heaven. For the rich, "It is easier for a camel to go through the eye of a needle than for a rich man to enter the kingdom of God" (Luke 18:25). He warns of striving to enter the narrow gate: "Strive to enter through the narrow gate, for many, I say to you, will seek to enter and will not be able" (Luke 18:17). He frequently warned of persecution, but also of this difficult entry into the Kingdom. He said to enter, one had to become like a child! "Truly I say to you, whoever does not receive the kingdom of God like a child shall not enter it at all" (Luke 13:24). As Paul, who accepted the call to spread the good news of the Kingdom, drew closer to his imminent departure, he warned his followers: "strengthening the souls of the disciples, encouraging them to continue in the faith, and saying, 'Through many tribulations we must enter the kingdom of God'" (Acts 14:22).

The common theme seems to be the great difficulty it is for people to set the Kingdom first in their lives in order to enter into it. A rich young ruler is busy with his riches, both of increasing and holding on to them (Luke 18:18). Becoming like a child means unless one believes and takes at face value the message of the Kingdom, this one will not enter. A child does not question what he or she is told, but trusts and remains joyful in most circumstances, and doesn't worry about the details of life. A child is pure—and we must become pure by the blood.

The narrow gate prevents many from entering. The broad path is what the world treads. Loaded down with burdens, cares, possessions and the quest for worldly pleasures, one cannot make it through a narrow gate, any more than a camel loaded with goods can enter a needle's eye.

Tribulations are a part of living in the world, and tribulations are especially part of kingdom living. Those with their eyes on the Kingdom sometimes experience normal financial pressures (exacerbated by the pressures of ministry if they make a living by the gospel), plus persecution, and in the face of adversity, must persevere to not lose sight of the goal. The Message translation of tribulation surrounding entrance into the Kingdom says:

> Putting muscle and sinew in the lives of the disciples, urging them to stick with what they had begun to believe and not quit, making it clear to them that it wouldn't be easy: "Anyone signing up for the kingdom of God has to go through plenty of hard times." (Acts 14:22 MSG)

The entire message of the gospel is, "Come." The good news of the Kingdom comes with a great invitation. Quoting from Isaiah, Paul says: "How beautiful are the feet of those who bring glad tidings of good things!" (Rom. 10:15b). The Targum comments on this verse from Isaiah:

> Go up on a high mountain, you prophets who bring good news to Zion! Lift up your voice in strength, you who bring good news to Jerusalem. Lift it up (and) do not fear. Say to the cities of the house of Judah:--"The kingdom of your God is revealed!" (Targum, Jonathan on Isa 40:9)

THE GREAT INVITATIONS

The biblical text tells us that Jesus was often invited to eat with those of rank in Jewish circles. On one such occasion as He brings the good news of the Kingdom, He teaches and because of one man's response to the Kingdom, Jesus directs a parable to Him. It is a striking account of a great invitation to enter the Kingdom, to which only few respond.

And one of those who reclined with Him heard these things, and he said to Him, "Blessed are those eating bread in the kingdom of God." And He said to him, "A certain man made a great supper and invited many. And he sent his servant at supper time to say to those who were invited, Come, for all things are now ready. And all with one consent began to make excuse. The first said to him, I have bought a piece of ground, I must go and see it. I beg you, have me excused. And another said, I have bought five yoke of oxen, and I am going to test them. I beg you, have me excused. And another said, I have married a wife, and therefore I cannot come. And coming up that servant reported these things to his lord. And the master of the house, being angry, said to his servant, Go out quickly into the streets and lanes of the city and bring in here the poor and the maimed, and the lame and the blind. And the servant said, Lord, it is done as you have commanded, and still there is room. And the lord said to the servant, Go out into the highways and hedges and compel them to come in, so that my house may be filled. For I say to you that none of these men who were invited shall taste of my supper." (Luke 14:15-24)

In this account, Jesus shows us that each must put the kingdom first, to set aside worldly concerns in favor of the Kingdom. While many professed to be in under God's reign, most were caught up in the issues of life. In this parable, each one invited has an excuse for why he cannot answer the summons. One was enamored with a purchase, having to look at a parcel of land—he was occupied with "the cares of this life." A second had a priority with training his oxen. The third flatly denied any way he could come since he had a new wife! This parallels other teachings of Jesus' about who was entering the Kingdom.

Matthew's gospel presents this same invitation as one to a wedding feast. The invitations require only that one answer the invitation by showing up. If you believe you are invited to a wedding supper, and your answer to this invitation is an answer to kingdom living, you would act. You would make preparations for the great feast and put on the garments provided by the Host. Garments represent the inner transformation, so to "put on" is to act wisely and walk uprightly with the empowerment of the Holy Spirit—a righteous way of living. One guest came but failed to put on the wedding garments. "Not everyone who says to Me, 'Lord, Lord,' will enter the kingdom of heaven; but he who does the will of My Father who is in heaven" (Matt. 7:21). Note the sages have a similar account that follows:

> All the reward intended for the righteous is ready for them in the world to come. And while they are yet in this world the Holy One, blessed be He!, lets them see the reward which he has prepared to give them in the world to come. And (their) souls are satisfied and they fall asleep. Rabbi Eleazar (ben Shammua') said:"(This) may be compared [mashal] to a king who arranged a banquet. He invited the guests and let them see what they would eat and drink, and they fell asleep. (Midrash, Bereshith Rabba 62.2)

Jesus gave a number of personal invitations that were refused as well as general invitations. Similar to the rich young ruler who went away sad because he was very rich and would not follow Jesus, another said, "Lord, let me first go and bury my father" (Luke 9:59). And another also said, "Lord, I will follow You, but let me first go and bid them farewell who are at my house" (Luke 9:61). The call may come unexpectedly at midnight, or at an inopportune time, will we answer?

Matthew gives an account of Jesus saying the social outcasts are entering the kingdom ahead of those who ought to come in first. He speaks of the main body of religious leaders not entering the kingdom, while the lower social order responds with repentance and obedience. It also speaks of those who say they are obedient, but are not, and those who are disobedient, but turn. One son says he will do what is asked, but doesn't. The other says he won't, but then does the will of his father. Jesus said to them, "Most certainly I tell you that the tax collectors and the prostitutes are entering into the Kingdom of God before you" (Mat 21:31). He even accuses them of trying to prevent others from entering. "Woe to you, lawyers! For you have taken away the key of knowledge. You did not enter in yourselves, and you have hindered those who were entering in" (Luke 11:52). Paul expresses what happens when we accept or refuse God's invitation: "Behold then the kindness and severity of God; to those who fell, severity, but to you, God's kindness, if you continue in His kindness; otherwise you also will be cut off" (Rom. 11:22). We are so blessed with His kindness and our entry into the Kingdom, but we must continue in His kindness, or experience His severity. His kindness leads us to repentance (Romans 2:4). He is the "Righteous Judge" (Psalm 7:11).

Because Jesus overcame, and we are in Him, in union with Him we can overcome the world. The world at that time was under Roman rule. Today, it is the world's system, and the evil that is throughout. When we are in the world, we are not of it. We are in God's kingdom. "Thy kingdom come, Thy will be done" is about the kingdom advancing. He is saying a parallelism; when His Kingdom comes, under God's rule, His will is being done!

REPENTANCE IS A KINGDOM KEY

The gospel Jesus preached required conversion. It is at the heart of His message. He said, "Assuredly, I say to you, unless you are **converted** and become as little children, you will by no means enter the kingdom of heaven" (Matt. 18:3). His reference to little children has to do with purity. The Jews considered little children to be pure. Leviticus is a book about purity and holiness, and the Jews taught it to their children first. The pure could digest the pure. It was as they grew that they had opportunities to yield to the flesh. To be **converted**, one has to become like a little child who is pure in heart. In the Jewish faith, repentance and baptism for repentance brought purity. John the Baptist's message was of repentance and baptism—"to prepare the way of the Lord." Hearts eager for the Messiah needed to be prepared to receive the Kingdom.

> *To be converted, one has to become like a little child who is pure in heart.*

Peter preached to those gathered in Jerusalem for Pentecost: "Repent therefore and be **converted**, that your sins may be blotted out, so that times of refreshing may come from the presence of the Lord" (Acts 3:19). According to the book of Acts, at his preaching, the disciples baptized over 3,000. Archeologists have uncovered a large complex of ritual immersion baths at the Temple site in Jerusalem.[4] Paul likewise preached repentance. Acts says: "So, being sent on their way by the church, they passed through Phoenicia and Samaria, describing the **conversion** of the Gentiles; and they caused great joy to all the brethren" (**Acts 15:3**). King David rejoiced in being cleansed of sin and sang, "Then I will teach transgressors Your ways, and sinners shall be **converted** to You" **(Psa 51:13)**. Conversion amounts to repenting, being baptized, and turning from sin to God. It is a matter of the heart.

Why is the believer's baptism in Jesus Christ as their Messiah so important? Number one, the Lord commanded it; and number two, it is at this point we come into contact with the blood of Christ. Baptism amounts to death. We are baptized into Christ's death, the blood cleanses us, and God raises us to new life in Christ (Romans 6:3). This is the "washing of regeneration and renewal by the Holy Spirit" (Titus 3:5).

Jesus taught his disciples that some will die as a result of life events, but repentance would avoid perishing. He is speaking as a prophet who warns Jerusalem of impending disaster, and He warns us today:

> Now on the same occasion there were some present who reported to Him about the Galileans, whose blood Pilate had mingled with their sacrifices. And He answered and said to them, "Do you suppose that these Galileans were greater sinners than all other Galileans, because they suffered this fate? **I tell you, no, but unless you repent, you will all likewise perish.** Or do you suppose that those eighteen on whom the tower in Siloam fell and killed them, were worse culprits than all

---

[4] Dr. Blizzard excavated the ritual immersion bath complex next to the monumental staircase just outside the temple walls in Jerusalem. The complex is so large that all 3,000 could have been baptized according to the Jewish method of ritual immersion in a short period of time on the day of Pentecost. Dr. Blizzard's material can be found at www.biblescholars.org.

the men who live in Jerusalem? **I tell you, no, but unless you repent, you will all likewise perish."** (Luke 13:1-5)

Jesus also said our repentance should produce acts of righteousness, and He warned that God is patient, but will not delay indefinitely. In mercy, He gives time to repent.

> Therefore **bring forth fruits in keeping with repentance**, and do not begin to say to yourselves, 'We have Abraham for our father,' for I say to you that God is able from these stones to raise up children to Abraham (Luke 3:8)
>
> Fertilize it and wait one more year, then cut down if no fruit. (Luke 13:6)
>
> It was planted in good soil beside abundant waters, that it might yield branches and bear fruit, and become a splendid vine. (Ezek 17:8)

When Jesus preached the Kingdom of Heaven, He couched His proclamation with repentance as the necessary prerequisite for entering. "Repent for the Kingdom of God is at hand" (Matt. 3:2, 4:17,10:7; Mark 1:14). Repentance amounts to a change of direction. It is turning from sin and a state of "lost-ness," from our ways to God's ways, from Self-rule to God's rule. We make a spiritual direction turn.

Forgiveness of sins is at the heart of the Gospel of the Kingdom. Jesus proclaimed: "That repentance for forgiveness of sins should be proclaimed in His name to all the nations, beginning from Jerusalem" (Luke 24:47). In obedience, Peter and those who followed preached, "Therefore let it be known to you, brethren, that through this Man is preached to you the forgiveness of sins" (Acts 5:15, Acts 13:38). He bought us the perfect redemption with His blood: "In Him we have redemption through His blood, the forgiveness of sins, according to the riches of His grace" (Eph 1:7). As the Second Adam,

Jesus lived a holy life, and in the redemption we have in Him, we exist in the new creation as though Adam never sinned!

When we repent and come into the Kingdom, we have committed to changing how we perceive and think. To repent and change means to "metamorphe." We begin to process thoughts and attitudes differently—from a righteous perspective. Anyone who repents (turns from sin and darkness to God) and is baptized, comes into contact with the blood of Christ Jesus, and receives the inward dwelling of the Spirit of God. A mere change of mind does not cover what all happens, but in the process of changing the thought processes of your mind—you refuse to accept thoughts of evil. Having been made righteous, having it imputed to us by the faithfulness of Christ Jesus, we take in things and deal with issues differently than we have before. We reject wrong thoughts and take them captive to the obedience of Christ (2 Cor 10:5).

Kingdom living requires a lifestyle of repentance—being a self-corrector: if we judge ourselves, we will not be judged (1 Cor 11:31). Throughout the epistles of Paul and the general epistles, Paul and others are correcting wrong thoughts and actions. Paul wanted the churches to remember the doctrine they were taught, to stop acting like mere men, and to live by the Spirit and walk by faith. He taught the kingdom. He warns and reproaches, and instructs. Most of the converts had little biblical training; therefore, they lacked the scriptures that showed men how to live uprightly.

FORGIVENESS IS A KINGDOM KEY

We know we should forgive even before anyone reminds us. Because of this, we will offer forgiveness, but we may struggle to stop the pain of offense. Recently, someone said something strongly to me in front of other people that shamed and embarrassed me. It stung! Even though the person later apologized, and I forgave with the words of my mouth, I was still angry. I spoke the word over myself, and again looked up scriptures to aid me. As I came to the well known passage, "forgive seven

> *Forgiveness is a Kingdom Key.*

times," I shuddered. I confessed to the Lord that I just did not know if I could go through what happened seven times in one day, and let it go. How do we "forgive from the heart" when we are perhaps shamed and stinging from harsh words?

Over the course of our lives, we will have many opportunities to withhold forgiveness. But Jesus said to "Be on guard!" We must be careful to avoid taking offense and withholding forgiveness. Jesus teaches how important forgiveness is in several places. The following text shows that it takes faith and love to forgive:

> And He said to His disciples, "It is inevitable that stumbling blocks should come, but woe to him through whom they come! It would be better for him if a millstone were hung around his neck and he were thrown into the sea, than that he should cause one of these little ones to stumble. Be on your guard! If your brother sins, rebuke him; and if he repents, forgive him. And if he sins against you seven times a day, and returns to you seven times, saying, 'I repent,' forgive him." And the apostles said to the Lord, "Increase our faith!" And the Lord said, "If you had faith like a mustard seed, you would say to this mulberry tree, 'Be uprooted and be planted in the sea'; and it would obey you. But which of you, having a slave plowing or tending sheep, will say to him when he has come in from the field, Come immediately and sit down to eat? But will he not say to him, Prepare something for me to eat, and properly clothe yourself and serve me until I have eaten and drunk; and afterward you will eat and drink? He does not thank the slave because he did the things which were commanded, does he? So you too, when you do all the things which are commanded you, say, 'We are unworthy slaves; we have done only that which we ought to have done.'" (Luke 17:1-10)

We are required to forgive, so like the unworthy slave, we must do what we ought and not look for any atta-boys; it is what we should do. Jesus quips, "And why do you not even on your own initiative judge what is right?" (Luke 12:57).

I find that an offense creates a debt, except this type of debt usually has emotional pain attached to it. Yet we have a strong incentive to forgive. Jesus said, "Forgive us our sins, for we ourselves also forgive everyone who is indebted to us. . ." (Luke 11:4). Obviously when we "judge what is right," and "do what we ought to have done," we refuse to hold someone indebted to us. When we forgive, we cancel their debt.

Jesus reminds us to rebuke a brother who sins, but if he asks for forgiveness, forgive. Even seven more times the same offense! No wonder the disciples said, "Increase our faith!"

In another story of forgiveness, Jesus tells of a man forgiving a servant who owed him ten thousand talents. The biblical text says, "The lord of that slave felt compassion and released him and forgave him the debt." But this slave was unwilling to forgive a fellow slave a small debt, and the lord got wind of it. "And his lord, moved with anger, handed him over to the torturers until he should repay all that was owed him. 'So shall My heavenly Father also do to you, if each of you does not forgive his brother from your heart'" (Luke 18:13-35). If we hold a person's debts against them until they pay, we are trying to extract "a pound of flesh." We are judging and condemning them, counting them unworthy of forgiveness. We have suffered so we want them to suffer! But God makes it clear that He is the one who judges righteously. We must leave vengeance to Him.

One method for "forgiving from the heart" is realizing how much we have been forgiven. If we imagine our debt—sins on the cross, we can see the offender's debt to us on the cross as well, and forgive the person. Forgiving the sin is not the answer; forgive the person. Most who sin against us are people we love. Because we love them, their offenses seem to sting the most. But we must see their offenses on the cross with our offenses, and forgive the person. We will be better for it.

We must be on guard against offense. The word "offense" is from "bait or trap." Offense then is a trap that can cause us to stumble. The best way to get over offense, even if it came from someone close to us, is to meditate on passages on forgiveness. One cause of pain is judging why someone spoke to us, and condemning them, which is wrong. People will mess up, but if we quit meditating on why they did it, then we can let go of the pain. We find from the scriptures above that forgiveness: is required of us, must be from the heart, releases the offender from debt, and heals our pain when we release the person. If forgiveness is from the heart, then it is with compassion and love.

I find that 1 Corinthians 13 is a great set of instructions on forgiveness as well as love. We must exercise love and faith to forgive. Just as the lord in the story, who forgave his servant ten thousand talents felt compassion, we must feel compassion and forgive. "Love is not provoked; Love takes no account for a wrong suffered, bears all things, believes all things, hopes all things, endures all things. Love never fails" (1 Cor 13:5, 7-8). We must see that God is love, and when we love, we forgive: "As He is so are we in the world" (1 John 4:17).

A dear friend read my notes on forgiveness and replied:

> Forgiveness is one of the ultimate acts of love. That is what Jesus did for us on the cross. Without asking why. If we can just love like He loved . . . He could have spent forever wondering why they beat Him and humiliated Him in public, why they did not believe Him, and why they spoke with hate towards Him when He had never done anything to them. He could have spent forever wondering and never gone to the cross. But He chose to forgive us all. If we could just forgive that one person and choose to love them and communicate with them in love, no matter what.

Therefore, in the words of the Lord's apostle Paul, "And be kind to one another, tender-hearted, forgiving each other, just as God in Christ also has forgiven you" (Ephes 4:32).

CHAPTER NINE

MYSTERIES OF THE KINGDOM

It is the glory of God to conceal a thing: but the glory of kings is to search it out. (Prov 25:2)

The Prophet Isaiah volunteers to prophesy to God's people after he beheld God's glory. Having realized his uncleanness and that of his people's whom he lived among, Isaiah cries, "For my eyes have seen the King, the LORD of hosts"(Isa 6:5b). When we have seen the glory of the Lord, we are changed forever. It happened to Moses, Isaiah, Ezekiel, Paul, and to some of us even in this day. In the mighty throne room in the Heavenlies, God asks whom He can send to His people. Isaiah responds, "Here am I, send me" (Isa 6:8b). God commands:

> Go! Say to these people: Keep listening, but do not understand; keep looking, but do not perceive. Dull the minds of these people; deafen their ears and blind their eyes; otherwise they might see with their eyes and hear with their ears, understand with their minds, turn back, and be healed. (Isaiah 6:9-10)

Jesus says something similar in several passages: "For this reason I speak to them in parables, because looking they do not see, and hearing they do not listen or understand" (Mat 13:13).

> So He said, "The secrets of the kingdom of God have been given for you to know, but to the rest it is in parables, so that looking they may not see, and hearing they may not understand. (Luke 8:10)

I do not believe we understand fully the reason Jesus spoke in parables. It relates to the people's hearts, their receptivity, and the process of hardening, of not perceiving and not hearing. Many times people quote the following verse as though Satan is able to blind people so they do not believe. Yes, he is able to deceive, and he works fulltime on believers in Christ to do just that—to lead them away from Christ. I know many who having once believed, have turned away from Christ.

Just as God commissioned Isaiah to speak and not see results, so Jesus spoke in parables and did not receive one hundred percent positive response. Only hearts open to receive heard. Paul speaks of this same principle in familiar terms:

> Regarding them: the god of this age has blinded the minds of the unbelievers so they cannot see the light of the gospel of the glory of Christ, who is the image of God. (2 Cor 4:4)

Blizzard responds to this verse:

> Here is the question: Why would it be necessary for the devil to blind the minds of those who did not believe, those who are already lost? Common sense should dictate that the devil would be busy trying to blind the minds of those who did believe. (Blizzard 2 Cor 4:3-4)[5]

The gospel of John contains a verse that is often used to parallel the above verse: "and concerning judgment, because the ruler of this age has been judged" (John 16:11). The Greek word for ruler is "*archisunagogos,*" and is also used in the sense of the ruler of a synagogue. It is not a reference to God, but of a ruling position. Paul picks up this theme again in Romans using verses from the Old Testament:

> Just as it is written, "GOD GAVE THEM A SPIRIT OF STUPOR, EYES TO SEE NOT AND EARS TO HEAR NOT, DOWN TO THIS VERY DAY." And David says, "LET THEIR TABLE BECOME A

---

[5] Dr. Blizzard's material can be found at www.biblescholars.org.

SNARE AND A TRAP, AND A STUMBLING BLOCK AND A RETRIBUTION TO THEM. LET THEIR EYES BE DARKENED TO SEE NOT, AND BEND THEIR BACKS FOREVER." (Rom. 11:8)

Paul adds, "But whenever a man turns to the Lord, the veil is taken away" (2 Cor 3:16). Many may have concluded in error that the "god of this world" is Satan, which is in opposition to monotheism. It points to a system of dualism, an Eastern Concept that has crept into Christianity. The verse should read, the "'God" of this age." God is over all. Satan may have some influence, but he is subject in every way to God. Age is the Greek word *aion* and in Hebrew *olam*. "One of the names for God used in Genesis 21:22" is 'El Olam'" (Blizzard 2 Cor 4:4). [6] Paul says God is over, through all and in all: "one God and Father of all who is over all and through all and in all" (Eph. 4:6); and again, "For from Him and through Him and to Him are all things" (Rom. 11:36). King David knew well the greatness of God. He says of Him, "For the LORD Most High is to be feared, A great King over all the earth" (Psa. 47:2); and, "That they may know that Thou alone, whose name is the LORD, Art the Most High over all the earth" (Psa. 83:18). Satan has no authority but what God allows Him for a season. "The LORD has established His throne in the heavens; And His sovereignty rules over all" (Psa. 103:19). Satan is not free to run amuck—he is limited by the One who is Sovereign. While we may engage in spiritual battle, and encounter an enemy of some power, we have been seated in Christ:

> Far above all rule and authority and power and dominion, and every name that is named, not only in this age, but also in the one to come. And He put all things in subjection under His feet, and gave Him as head over all things to the church, which is His body, the fullness of Him who fills all in all. And raised us up with Him, and seated us with Him in the heavenly places, in Christ Jesus. (Eph 1:21-23, 2:6)

---

[6] Dr. Blizzard's material can be found at www.biblescholars.org.

You will recall in **Chapter Two**, the Greek word for age is *aion*, which represents a period of time. So "the God of this age," is also the "God of the age to come!" Adam Clarke tells us that many of the early believers of some authority believed the contested verse refers to the "God" of this age, and not "god." He writes,

> I must own I feel considerable reluctance to assign the epithet o qeoß, THE God, to Satan; and were there not a rooted prejudice in favour of the common opinion, the contrary might be well vindicated, viz. that by the God of this world the supreme Being is meant, who in his judgment gave over the minds of the unbelieving Jews to spiritual darkness, so that destruction came upon them to the uttermost. Satan, it is true, has said that the kingdoms of the world and their glory are his, and that he gives them to whomsoever he will; Matt. iv. 8, 9. But has God ever said so? And are we to take this assertion of the boasting devil and father of lies for truth? Certainly not. We are not willing to attribute the blinding of men's minds to God, because we sometimes forget that he is the God of justice, and may in judgment remove mercies from those that abuse them; but this is repeatedly attributed to him in the Bible. Irenaeus, Tertullian, Chrysostom, Theodouret, Photius, Theophylact, and Augustine, (early church fathers) all plead for the above meaning; and St. Augustine says that it was the opinion of almost all the ancients. (Clarke "2 Cor 4:4)

The belief in a Messiah is deeply rooted in the Jewish faith. However, not all the Jews who believed Messiah would come received Christ as their Messiah. Jesus exclaims, "You have your heads in your Bibles constantly because you think you'll find eternal life there. But you miss the forest for the trees. These Scriptures are all about *me*!" (John 5:39 MSG). Unbelief hinders God's work in the world, and it hardens hearts. Faith is always just that: faith. It means a choice is always available to believe and come out of a state of being lost and enter into life. To not see is to remain in blindness and in a lost state.

When one does not accept truth by faith, then the heart becomes more hardened, and God blinds the unbeliever—Exodus tells us that God "hardened" Pharaoh's heart! I would think that Satan wants to blind, and bring to unbelief, those who are saved, those who do see. He has no need to blind those who do not believe, since they are already blinded. Once someone chooses to not believe in Christ, it seems that God blinds them. **But remember, they are already unbelievers before God blinds them.** They hear but do not understand. They see but do not perceive. Still God speaks to them. Jesus speaks in parables because they do not see and do not listen.

> *Were we to understand while in unbelief, and not turn, we would be forever lost and in sin.*

The theme of what God spoke to Isaiah, and Jesus to His followers is that God does not give revelation on what we do not have a heart to understand. He does not give "pearls to swine." He allows Satan to steal it from those without the heart for it. Sound strange, but were we to receive the word of the Kingdom in a lost state of unbelief, we would have refused what could have saved us. Whatever man refuses and turns to in lieu of salvation, God gives him over to that. Here is the point, were we to understand while in unbelief, and not turn, we would be forever lost and in sin. Jesus makes a point with those who do not believe, "If you were blind, you would have no sin; but since you say, 'We see,' your sin remains." (John 9:4). It was a reminder of a verse in Jeremiah: "Yet you said, 'I am innocent; Surely His anger is turned away from me.' Behold, I will enter into judgment with you because you say, 'I have not sinned'" (Jer 2:35). The moment one turns from unbelief to Christ, revelation comes, salvation comes, and "the veil is taken away."

> *The theme of what God spoke to Isaiah, and Jesus to His followers is that God does not give revelation on what we do not have a heart to understand.*

PARABLE OF THE SOWER

In the parable of the sower, the Kingdom key of receptivity is again revealed. To those who believe and have a heart to understand, he explains His message and they understand. But those who do not believe, nor have a heart to understand, then his message is not understood. The message of the Kingdom when preached and received in an honest heart, will produce fruit. Words are seeds, giving is a seed, loving is a seed, acts of kindness are seeds, and seeds will produce if planted and given light and water. They are programmed to produce. If a seed does not produce, the problem is in the soil—the heart. The amazing parable of the sower is about how the Kingdom operates, how it is grown, and how the message of the Kingdom can fall on hearts not ready to receive, and thus likewise, fail to produce fruit. We often apply this teaching to sowing and reaping in the realm of money (and the principle of sowing and reaping is a real one), but Jesus is speaking purely about receiving the salvation of the Kingdom in the parable of the sower:

> *Jesus is speaking purely about receiving the salvation of the Kingdom in the parable of the sower.*

> And His disciples began questioning Him as to what this parable might be. And He said, "To you it has been granted to know the mysteries of the kingdom of God, but to the rest it is in parables, in order that seeing they may not see, and hearing they may not understand. Now the parable is this: the seed is the word of God. And those beside the road are those who have heard; then the devil comes and takes away the word from their heart, so that they may not believe and be saved. And those on the rocky soil are those who, when they hear, receive the word with joy; and these have no firm root; they believe for a while, and in time of temptation fall away. And the seed which fell among the thorns, these are the ones who have heard, and as they go on their way they are choked with worries and riches and pleasures of this life, and bring no fruit to maturity. And the seed in the good soil, these are the ones who have heard the word in an honest and good heart, and hold it fast, and bear fruit with perseverance. (Luke 8:9-15)

At first glance this parable sounds unfair. It appears that some seed had no opportunity to grow. It was scattered aimlessly. Yet when we understand that in that day the plowing came after the sowing, we can see this is not the case. Jesus uses seed in the sense of each of His teachings about the Kingdom are as seeds that can take root and grow. The sower sows seeds, the Word of the Kingdom of God, and Satan cannot steal a word from someone with an honest and good heart, who by persevering will not let go of it.

Jesus said this parable had to do with the Kingdom, in believing and being saved. The object is to hear the word, believe with an honest and good heart and be saved—delivered, set free, removed from danger, healed and made whole—become a part of Jesus' Kingdom movement. Those who hear with an honest and good heart, and persevere by doing the word will bear fruit. Seeds beside the road have fallen on unreceptive hearts. The message of salvation does not come into their heart, and they are targets for Satan's thievery. They "have heard" though. Seeds that fall among the rocks represent a heart without room for the message of salvation to send down deep roots. The soil, the heart and mind are shallow—never having grasped the depth of God's love that He wants to demonstrate through Messiah. This type of heart is more interested in displaying right standing with God by works, rather than receiving by faith. Another type of heart has let "the cares of this life and deceitfulness of riches" choke the seed of the Kingdom.

> *Whether you want to call it "cause and effect," "giving and receiving, or "sowing and reaping," it is a Kingdom principle.*

Once more Jesus is pointing to the necessity of doing what God says. Jesus wants His teachings to be performed! He adds:

> "Now no one after lighting a lamp covers it over with a container, or puts it under a bed; but he puts it on a lampstand, in order that those who come in may see the light. For nothing is hidden that shall not become evident, nor anything secret that shall not be known and come to light. Therefore take care how you listen; for whoever has, to him shall more be given; and whoever does not have, even what he thinks he has shall be taken away from him." And His mother and brothers came to Him, and they were unable to get to Him because of the crowd. And it was reported to Him, "Your mother and

Your brothers are standing outside, wishing to see You." But He answered and said to them, "My mother and My brothers are these who hear the word of God and do it." (Luke 8:16-21)

We are so blessed to have the words of Jesus preserved for us, and the Spirit of God to make them real to us. He brings revelation. Jesus was pleased to share the mysteries to His disciples, and to us today:

At that very time He rejoiced greatly in the Holy Spirit, and said, "I praise Thee, O Father, Lord of heaven and earth, that Thou didst hide these things from the wise and intelligent and didst reveal them to babes. Yes, Father, for thus it was well-pleasing in Thy sight. (Luke 10:21)

Measure for Measure

Jesus discusses receiving "measure for measure" a number of times in the gospels. Whether you want to call it "cause and effect," "giving and receiving," or "sowing and reaping," it is a Kingdom principle. Often as I read on Kingdom living in the gospels, I am amazed at how all is about sowing and reaping. What we sow, we reap—cause and effect—measure for measure.

Bearing fruit amounts to being a "doer of the Word." Jesus said it in many ways, "the doer of the word is blessed, my mother and brothers are those who hear and do, the one who builds his house on a rock is the one who is a doer of the word, why do you call me Lord and do you not do what I say?"

The principle of sowing and reaping can also apply not only to salvation, but to *tzedakah*, righteousness demonstrated in charity and acts of kindness. Recall that salvation and righteousness are interchangeable words in Hebrew. God rewards "measure for measure" so we can expect our giving to be a righteous expression of Kingdom living. When Jesus says what we call the golden rule, "Do unto others what you would have them do unto you," He is expressing "measure for measure." This was a rabbinic expression as was the concept of doing for others what we would have them do unto us. If we give mercy, we can expect mercy, if we judge, we can expect to be judged, and if we would but love our enemies, we would be imitating God, "who sends rain on the righteous and the unrighteous" (Matt 5:45).

> *If we would but love our enemies, we would be imitating God, "who sends rain on the righteous and the unrighteous."*

CONCLUSION

THE MASTER KEY—COVENANT OF THE KINGDOM

I no longer call you servants; I call you friends

Throughout this look at the Kingdom of Heaven, you find references to the Covenant. I have described it as a part of what God gives to us along with eternal life, an entrance into the world to come, and a great inheritance. We enter the Kingdom and into Covenant. It seemed I heard the Lord say, "The Master Key–Covenant of the Kingdom." I first wrote of Covenant in an earlier book, *"Types and Shadows."* Of course, our knowledge of God is a fluid process, and over the years, He led me into more truth. I do believe He inspired this former work in a chapter on Covenant, so I present portions of it as follows:

"Covenant can be only understood in light of its significance to those involved—a binding contract between two parties that makes them as one, each pledging an everlasting union of friendship. The entire life of each party is bound up in the life of the other, including their families, possessions, and their mutual protection. This should describe our relationship with God. My own heart's cry to God has been to become the kind of friend that He could count faithful and quick to obey, someone of whom He could ask anything. Would others say of us what Abigail said to King David, as she attempted to sway David from revenge: ". . . Your God-honored life is tightly bound in the bundle of God-protected life" (1 Samuel 25:29 MSG). She knew David valued and honored God in Covenant.

A covenant is always ratified with blood. The blood that flows together from each party is symbolic of the union of covenant friendship. One portion of a dictionary definition of covenant defines it's meaning as "to come; a coming together" (Webster "Covenant"). This is the meaning of the covenant God made with Abraham. Of course, God being the greater party in the covenant, He stands able and willing to bless in greater measure and fulfill His promises. In the book of Hebrews, we read, "In which it is impossible for God to lie" (Hebrews 6:18). Writes Andrew Murray,

Amid all delay and disappointment, and apparent failure of the Divine Promises, the covenant was to be the anchor of the soul, pledging the Divine veracity and faithfulness and unchangeableness for the certain performance of what had been promised. (Murray 14)

Who at one time has not desired a good friend? But how about "a friend that sticks closer than a brother?" (Proverbs 18:24). The Hebrew word for friend in this verse is *ahab*. It means to be a friend in an intimate sense (Strong 157). A clue for fully understanding this Hebrew root word is to look at its uses elsewhere in the Bible. This same word is used to describe God's relationship with Abraham. "But thou, Israel, my servant, Jacob whom I have chosen, the seed of Abraham my friend . . . " (Isaiah 41:8). God made covenant with Abraham and became His friend. The friend that sticks closer than a brother is the blood brother—the blood-covenant-intimate Friend.

After He had finished the Passover meal, and spoke of the New Covenant in His blood, Jesus used the word friend to describe His relationship with His disciples. "I no longer call you servants . . . I call you friends" (John 15:15). To be sure the friendship commitment sealed in His blood was an everlasting one, He also asked the Father to send us a friend to be with us forever—the Spirit of Truth, who is to be with us and in us (John 14:16-17). The Holy Spirit is the seal or sign of Covenant.

> *The Holy Spirit is the seal or sign of Covenant.*

In the case of Covenant between God and man, God is holy and cannot have union where sin is present. Even though He may love the person, sin would cause the other party to be consumed by His holiness. Death is the result. He must therefore, see that the man with whom He binds himself in union is purified of any offense, and effect reconciliation. A sacrifice is substituted to die for the life of the one whom God chooses to bless with His Covenant of friendship.

Oh The Blood!

The Hebrew word for covenant is *berith*. Some definitions signify that it means to cut a compact; a league of friendship, or cut until blood flows as in a treaty (Strong 1254, Brown-Driver-Briggs 1285). A person or a substitute is required for the blood to flow; therefore, covenant also includes the idea of a binding agreement of friendship between parties that is sealed by a sacrifice of some nature in which blood flows from a cut. You may think of it as a binding together by shedding blood through a sacrifice. Adam Clarke writes, "*Berith* signifies not only a covenant, but also the sacrifice offered on the occasion" (Clarke Genesis 6:18).

Why a bloody sacrifice to make covenant and bring the other person into this binding relationship with God? It is a great mystery. God is outside of time. I heard the Spirit say, "Time is His vehicle for accomplishing His plan." I believe that He looked down through the eons of time and saw that man would need to have His own divine nature to overcome the effects of sin. The Old Covenant served as a temporary means for atonement. Isaiah 53 prophesied of the Messiah's atoning sacrifice, and the Old Testament sacrifices shadowed it. The New Testament reveals the eternal covenant in the blood of Christ, God's own Son (Hebrews 13:20). God would place such a value on the blood of Christ that it would serve to reconcile the entire world—its value so much greater than that of the animal substitutes used in the Shadow Christology of animal sacrifices. Writes Murray,

> The blood is one of the strangest, the deepest, the mightiest, and the most heavenly of the thoughts of God. It lies at the very root of both Covenants, but especially of the New Covenant. The difference in the two Covenants is the difference between the blood of beasts, and the blood of the Lamb of God. The power of the New Covenant has no lesser measure than the worth of the blood of the Son of God! (Murray 75,76).

God chose the medium of blood for demonstrating the life of the animal, its blood, was given as a substitute for the life of the person receiving "expiation," a turning away of God's wrath, so that the person could draw near. Future generations would see blood and the sacrifice in the same light. The blood provided the expiation. Bible expositors write, "God had set apart the blood, as the medium of expiation for the human soul, for the altar, i.e., to be sprinkled upon the altar" (Keil and Delitzsch "Leviticus 17:11").

As earlier mentioned, the blood was the medium or the symbol of life. The life of the animal was given and each party committed their lives to the other—even unto death if the vows were broken. It also served to reconcile man to His God. The Bible says, "For the life of an animal is in the blood. I have provided the blood for you to make atonement for your lives on the Altar; it is the blood, the life, that makes atonement" (Leviticus 17:11 MSG).

God made covenant with the "whole creation" through Noah, and gave the rainbow as a sign of the Covenant (Genesis 9:12-13). The covenant God made with Abraham, with circumcision as the sign, was "to him and his descendents" after him (Genesis 17:7). God's covenant with Moses is identified "with Israel," and included observance of God's law (Exodus 19:5). But it included any foreigner that would join himself or herself to God and observe the ordinances, even those whom He might graft in at a later time. The Bible says, "In future generations, when a foreigner or visitor living at length among you presents a Fire-Gift as a pleasing fragrance to GOD, the same procedures must be followed" (Numbers 15:14 MSG).

The sign of this New Covenant in the Lord Jesus is in the circumcision of hearts and the gift of the Holy Spirit (Romans 2:29). Jesus described beforehand what He would do for those who believed in Him. "He did the same with the cup after supper, and said, "This cup is the New Covenant in my blood poured out for you" (Luke 22:20). God's New Covenant through Jesus Christ, the bloody sacrificial substitute, is to "whosoever" will by faith receive Him (Romans 4:1-5). The Holy Spirit is our seal, our sign of covenant.

COVENANT INHERITANCE

One of God's chief purposes in Covenant is to bring us to trust Him completely, such that we have total dependence on Him. This is a love relationship, the doting love of a Father for His children. One of the most amazing and the greatest benefits of covenant is becoming a child of God. John says, "But to those who did accept Him He gave power to become children of God" (John 1:12). God wants us to become One with Him, and bestow on us the many blessings He stored up for us in Christ. One of the love letters written to us through John says, "See how great a love the Father has bestowed on us, that we would be called children of God" (1 John 3:1). Murray explains, "The New Covenant may become to us one of the windows of heaven through which we see into the face, into the very heart of God" (Murray 17).

The New Covenant comes to us through inheritance—the death of the one who is bequeathing an inheritance, Jesus Christ. "For where a testament is, there must of necessity be the death of him that made it" (Hebrews 9:16). We were grafted into the vine of Christ (Romans 11:17). The New Covenant is made "for us" and not "with us." God made covenant with Jesus Christ, who acted on our behalf.

Someone told the story of a young girl in another country who was going to attend services not sanctioned by the State. When stopped by a patrol on Sunday morning on her way to services and interrogated, she said, "My elder brother has died, and I am going to the reading of the will." This portrays our position. In Christ we are inheritors, "blessed with every spiritual blessings in the heavenly places" (Ephesians 1:3) (Christian 41-47).

The Master Key is the Covenant of the Kingdom. It is about our divine friendship and relationship with the King. We are not mere subjects, we are One with Him through the blood of the eternal Covenant. In the words of Paul, "For you have died and your life is hidden with Christ in God" (Col 3:3). We died, and God made us alive with Christ. We are one body; He is the head, but we are connected in One Spirit. "God is Spirit" (John 4:24). The biblical text says, "For by one Spirit we were all baptized into one body, whether Jews or Greeks, whether slaves or free, and we were all made to drink of one Spirit" (1Cor. 12:13); "But the one who joins himself to the Lord is one spirit with Him" (1 Cor 6:17).

> *The Master Key is the Covenant of the Kingdom.*

Those who died in faith looked forward to the day in which God would act to fulfill His promises (Heb. 11:13). God made annual atonement for Israel and passed over their sins through sacrifices. Yet these all looked forward to the one sacrifice Jesus would make. No one was justified apart from Him:

Whom God displayed publicly as a propitiation in His blood through faith. This was to demonstrate His righteousness, because in the forbearance of God He passed over the sins previously committed; for the demonstration, I say, of His righteousness at the present time, that He might be just and the justifier of the one who has faith in Jesus. (Romans 3:25-26)

Because God had provided something better for us, so that apart from us they should not be made perfect. (Heb. 11:40)

THE KINGDOM "KEYLESS ENTRY"

If you purchase a new car, you may find that all you need is to enter a code or have your car keys in your purse or pocket, and the door opens and your car starts without a key. Or maybe to enter your garage without a door opener, you have a touch pad to raise the door. Keyless entries are a wonderful invention. In Christ, we have something far more wonderful. In Christ, we have a keyless entry into the Kingdom, Covenant, and the very Throne Room of God. His blood is recognized as the code to enter boldly.

No more does a curtain divide the Holy of Holies from the rest of the rooms of God. When Christ died, God tore the Temple veil in half. Human hands could not accomplish removing this barrier to intimacy, only God, in the person of Jesus Christ, whose alone blood qualified. A mere man's blood would not give us what we needed. As slaves to sin, we were unable to redeem ourselves. We needed more than a man; we needed Messiah who God

> *The "Keyless Entry" into the Throne Room is the Blood of Jesus.*

conceived with His Holy Blood by the Holy Spirit. This blood bought the church, the witnessing body of believers ". . . shepherd the church of God which He purchased with His own blood" (Acts 20:28).

When we die Christ's death in the waters of baptism, we come into contact with the very blood of God through Christ and receive new Spiritual DNA, becoming new creatures (a totally new species). We have a keyless entry. The Book of Hebrews say, "By virtue of the blood of Jesus, you and I . . . May now have confidence to enter the Holy Place by a fresh and living way" (Hebrews 10:19-20). We may go directly to our Father, birthed anew by His blood through Christ, having our sins forgiven and our hearts sprinkled clean by His blood. Hebrews continues, "Let us draw near with a sincere heart in full assurance of faith, having our hearts sprinkled clean from an evil conscience and our bodies washed with pure water" (Heb. 10:22). Those who went before us could only enter with a sacrifice to worship, the meaning of "draw near." We have full confidence that we are able to draw near boldly because we are washed (baptized) into His death and our hearts sprinkled clean by His blood. Our "hearts" means our entire inner being.

  A covenant is a promise that cannot be broken if it is a promise by God. The Master Covenant Key shows us that in connection with our Great Friend, the Kingdom of Heaven is to advance through us, the body of Christ, until its ultimate fulfillment. The Kingdom of Heaven is an eternal dimension of the Spirit, and we are united in One Spirit with the King forever through Covenant—set apart for eternity. We receive His blood, and are members of His Covenant Body.

BIBLIOGRAPHY

Blizzard, Dr. Roy. Articles and Verses in Translation on Bible Scholars, Inc: Dr. Blizzard's material can be found at www.biblescholars.org. Used by permission.

Christian, Dr. Shirley, Types and Shadows, Prophetic Pictures of Wholeness in Christ. Xulon Press: 2006. Used by permission.

Dead Sea Scrolls, Thanksgiving Hymns (1QH). (Electronic Datasource)

Flusser, David. Jesus. Hebrew University Magness Press; Jerusalem, 1997, 2001.

Hagin, Kennth E. The Triumphant Church. Rhema Bible Church, Broken Arrow, OK, 1993. Used by permission.

Murray, Andrew. The Two Covenants. Uhrichsville, OH: Barbour and Company, Inc., MVMXCVI.

Stern, David, Jewish New Testament Commentary. Clarksville, Maryland, Jewish New Testament Publications, 1979. Quotations are taken from the Jewish New Testament Commentary, copyright © 1979 by David H. Stern. Published by Jewish New Testament Publications, Inc. www.messianicjewish.net/jntp. Distributed by Messianic Jewish Resources. www.messianicjewish.net. All rights reserved. Used by permission.

JewishEncyclopedia.com. Copyright 2002, Public Domain.

Strong, James. Strong's Exhaustive Concordance of the Bible. World Bible Publishers, Inc., 1986.

Unless otherwise indicated, all scripture quotations are from the New American Standard Bible®, copyright© 1960, 1962, 1963, 1968, 1971, 1972, 1973, 1975, 1977, 1995 by the The Lockman Foundation. Used by permission.

Scriptures taken from the New Jerusalem Bible are indicated as NJB. New York, NY: Doubleday, 1958.

Scripture references marked AMP are taken from The Amplified Bible, Old Testament copyright 1965,1987 by the Zondervan Corporation. The Amplified New Testament copyright 1958, 1987 by The Lockman Foundation, 1958-1987.

Scripture references marked MSG are taken from the Message Remix: The Bible in Contemporary Language, Eugene Peterson, NavPress Publishing Group, 2003.

Green, Jay P. Modern King James Version (MKJV). Copyright © 1962.

Scriptures marked as HCSB are taken from the Holman Christian Standard Bible. Nashville, Tennesee: Holman Bible Publishers, 2000.

New International Version (NIV). Copyright © 1973, 1978, 1984 by International Bible Society. Used by Permission.

Brown, F., Driver, S., Briggs, C. Brown-Driver-Briggs Hebrew and English Lexicon. Electronic Database.

Clarke, Adam. The Holy Bible with a Commentary and Critical Notes. 6 vols. New York: G. Lane & C.B. Tippett, 1837-1847.

Keil, Karl F., and F. Delitzsch. Biblical Commnetary on the Old Testament. 25 vols. Grand Rapids: Wm. B. Eerdmans, 1949-1955.

"From the days of John the Baptist until now the Kingdom of Heaven is breaking through, and those who break through seize it' (Matthew 11:12).

ASSURANCE OF SALVATION

If you are not confident about your eternal home, or have any doubt as to your peace with God, then pray this prayer out loud:

Father,

I repent of my sins, and I ask you to forgive me and cleanse me by the blood of Jesus Christ. Your Word says that *if I confess with my mouth Jesus as Lord, and believe in my heart that God raised Him from the dead, I will be saved,* according to Romans 10:9. I believe Jesus died for me and rose from the dead. Through the blood of Jesus, I believe I am free, according to Ephesians 1:7. I believe I have eternal life according to John 3:16, and that I do not come into judgment, but out of death into life, according to John 5:24. Please confirm your love to me now by giving me supernatural love, joy, and peace. I pray in Jesus name. Amen.

ABOUT THE AUTHOR

Dr. Shirley Christian actively fulfills a role of instruction and oversight in Lubbock, Texas as International Dean and Professor of Biblical Studies of Harvest Ministry Seminary. Her many years of ministry in a healing school with the gifts of the Spirit in operation, and the things she had gone through personally, worked a deep compassion within her for the lost and hurting. The Holy Spirit entrusted Shirley with a strong intercessory prayer life, healing and prophetic giftings, and through her brings truth and deliverance to the Body of Christ. Shirley flows in streams of His grace, streams of intercession, cleansing, healing and revelation.

The Holy Spirit inspired the motto, Streams of His Grace, for Shirley Christian Ministries during a time of prayer. Shirley believes the inspiration for the motto is based on how the Holy Spirit manifests His presence in streams of revelation, power and intercession.

If you enjoyed <u>Unseen Realities of God's Kingdom</u> by Dr. Shirley Christian, please visit the ministry website for other products and books such as <u>Types and Shadows, Prophetic Pictures of Wholeness in Christ</u>, <u>Living the Fasted Life</u>, <u>Cleansing and Healing Streams,</u> and <u>Keys to a Sound Mind.</u> You will also find free downloads of teaching and confession CDs on her ministry website:

www.shirleychristian.org

www.ingramcontent.com/pod-product-compliance
Lightning Source LLC
Chambersburg PA
CBHW020010050426
42450CB00005B/402